Healing the
Scars of
Emotional
Abuse

Healing the Scars of Emotional Abuse

Gregory L. Jantz

Fleming H. Revell
A Division of Baker Book House Co
Grand Rapids, Michigan 49516

Published by Fleming H. Revell
a division of Baker Book House Company
P.O. Box 6287, Grand Rapids, MI 49516-6287

Second printing, April 1996

Printed in the United States of America

Library of Congress Cataloging-in-Publication Data

Jantz, Gregory L.
    Healing the scars of emotional abuse / Gregory L. Jantz.
       p.   cm.
    ISBN 0-8007-5556-1
    1. Psychological abuse. I. Title.
    RC569.5.P75J36   1995
    616.85'2—dc20
                                    94-36792

To protect the privacy of those involved, names have been changed in all of the case studies used in this book.

This book is dedicated to those who have lost hope and are struggling with the painful void created by unmet emotional needs. You have a future and a hope!

Contents

Acknowledgments

M any people shared in the birth of this book, and I gratefully acknowledge those who have contributed significantly to it. My publisher, Bill Petersen, gave me the opportunity to usher life into the manuscript. Among those to whom I owe special gratitude are: my wife, La Fon, who co-founded The Center for Counseling & Health Resources, Inc. and has been faithful to the calling of our vision together; Rich Hurst, our dear friend, who has encouraged us from the beginning and offered us wisdom and a sense of perspective; our God-given staff, who patiently and prayerfully persevered with me. I am grateful for the academic scholarship, suggestions, and encouragement from Dr. Richard Crews. Sincere appreciation goes to Ann McMurry, my collaborator, who spent hundreds of hours arranging my material and presenting it in an organized, concise literary form. Ann captured my heart and vision for this project. La Fon and I have had many faithful friends and family who have prayed for us and our work over the years. We have been blessed by each of you.

Part One

Understanding
Emotional
Abuse

What Is Emotional Abuse?

David was eighteen years old when he killed himself. He was never physically beaten or sexually molested by anyone, yet David was the victim of abuse. At the time no one put that name on it. His death was tragic, certainly, but no one ever stopped to think about his life. David died as a result of lifelong emotional abuse. Continual, pervasive, easily denied and overlooked emotional abuse.

David's father had been a football player all through school. He had the same dream for his son. There was just one problem. He never stopped long enough in his pursuit of athletic excellence for his son to ask David if *he* wanted to be a football player. He just assumed David would want to excel in sports as he had.

As expected, David played football growing up. In fact, he excelled at it, being physically large and strong for his age. It was even fun at first—the roar of the crowd, the overwhelming attention lavished on him by his family, the obvious pride others took in his athletic ability. But the pressure to succeed, to live up to his father's expectations, was tremendous. As time went on, no matter how well David did, there was always another level to reach, more he still had to do. No longer was David competing against another team or against other children; instead, he was competing against his father's expectations of how much he had accomplished (or thought he had) at the same age.

Eventually the pressure got so intense David could no longer cope. When he was fifteen, he tried to kill himself. The attempt failed, but the injuries he suffered because of the attempt left him unable to compete in sports. David had ingested a common poison that settled into his joints, weakening them so that sports was now totally out of the question. Even though he was still alive, David thought he was off the hook. Maybe now his father would stop trying to force him to be a football player and would listen to what David really wanted to be—an artist.

The pressure to compete in sports did indeed stop, but so did everything else. David became the invisible person in the family. No longer the focus of his father's sports ambition, David found there was no other place for him in the family. David's sister, Janice, became the athlete of the family. Built strong, like David, she excelled in two sports: track and field and gymnastics. She lettered in both sports in high school and competed at the state level. David's role diminished steadily, outshined by the light of his sister's athletic prowess.

Completely convinced of his own worthlessness, David gradually lost all hope of ever recapturing his father's attention. His exceptional artistic ability and vision were not valued in his family. Because of his lack of performance, his birthright had been passed to his younger sister.

One spring day, during one of Janice's high school track meets, David escaped to his room. Determined to be successful this time, he shot himself in the head.

When news of his death became known, everyone agreed it was a terrible tragedy. But then they all remembered, shaking their heads, that he'd tried it once before. He always had been a messed up kid. David's inability to cope with life was attributed to some tragic defect in his personality. No one ever stopped to consider that David had been abused all his life. He'd never been beaten or molested, but David died of abuse—emotional abuse. Leaving no marks, it still left him dead.

As a professional counselor treating eating disorders for over ten years, I've become very concerned about the often overlooked issue of emotional abuse. For many years I have noticed that the focus of abuse, even the concept of abuse, has centered around the physical beatings, outward neglect, and sexual invasion of children. The signs of emotional abuse, however, are easier to overlook. There is no scar tissue to stretch, no bruises to yellow and heal, no gaping wound to point to. In spite of their invisibility, emotional wounds comprise a very damaging form of abuse.

While emotional abuse always accompanies physical and sexual abuse, it can also be present on its own. Because its implications have been overlooked, it's been left to do its damage in silence. The abused have no recourse but to wonder why they just can't seem to get their lives on track. Each will think back to his or her childhood and won't be able to come up with a single time Dad backhanded him across the room or Mom left her alone for days at a time with no food, or a cousin wanted to do "naughty" things behind the house when the adults weren't looking. These people conclude, therefore, they were never abused and delve no further into their past to discover why their present doesn't seem to be working.

Though harder to spot, emotional abuse is easier to deny. But just as physical and sexual abuse have signposts to mark their presence, emotional abuse, being a systematic attack on one's sense of self, has common traits. Just as physical and sexual abuse come in degrees of severity, emotional abuse runs the gamut of intensity and damage.

All of us have, at one time or another, come under attack by people who just happen to be having a bad day. They take out their frustrations on us, and we feel battered by the winds of their emotions. We've all had it happen to us, and we've all probably been guilty of it a time or two. No one is perfect, and all of us slip up and occasionally say things or do things we know we shouldn't. That's normal.

Emotional abuse isn't normal. Emotional abuse is the consistent pattern of being treated unfairly and unjustly, over a period of time, usually by the same person or people. It can also be a onetime traumatic event that is left unresolved.

It's the mother who yells in frustration every time her son makes a mistake, "Why can't you be more like your sister?" Or the father who snorts in derision as he proclaims regularly to everyone who will listen, "This kid won't amount to *nothing!*" It's the husband who tells his wife, "You're too stupid to get a job!"

Like other forms of abuse, emotional abuse can be self-perpetuating, repeating the cycle over and over again, throughout relationships and across generations. If emotional abuse has occurred early in life, it can cause dysfunctional behavior into the adult years.

It is important to understand that abuse has a broad definition as well as broad effects. While physical and sexual abuse can be much more visible and therefore considered more severe, it is vital not to measure abuse on a scale of "bad" to "worse." Rather, it is important to acknowledge its presence, whether in the past or the present.

So many of the people I have counseled over the years started out by telling me, "It's not like I was abused or anything. . . ." They then proceeded to recount horror stories of growing up with what I strongly believe is emotional abuse. Too often they seemed embarrassed as they talked, as if making too big a deal out of what happened to them. Attempting to minimize their abuse is one of the chief denial techniques developed to emotionally survive through childhood.

So how do you know if you've been abused in the past or if the relationship you're in now is an abusive one? Often you aren't the best judge. If you've grown up in an abusive family, it will all have a bizarre sense of normalcy. If you compare your abusive past with a current abusive relationship and vice versa, there will appear to be nothing different to point to the reality of abuse.

However, even if you're not the *best* judge, you are really the *only* judge. In my counseling, I've found that when people think they were abused, they were. If the relationship you had in the past or the one you have now is with a person or people who consistently make you feel worthless, you're being abused. All of us need relationships with people who love us, who build us up, and who support us as we learn and grow.

Of course, not all relationships are perfect, and things can be said or done in anger that are regretted later. But if those things are a pattern, if they are used to degrade and control, no matter how subtle they may seem or how much the other person tells you they are really for "your own good," in truth they are abuse. You may be asking yourself, "Where does constructive criticism end and abuse take over?" This book is designed to help you identify the signs and common types of emotional abuse and to know what to do about it.

Emotional abuse by itself or used in conjunction with physical or sexual abuse can be easy to recognize if you know what to look for. Many of the types of abuse identified in this book will take the form of a message—the spoken and unspoken messages passed on to you as a child that constitute the basic structure of your self-identity and self-esteem. These messages, either positive or negative, have become incorporated into how you feel about yourself. Adults as well as children can be emotionally abused, but in each case the messages were meant to belittle, to devalue, to shame, and ultimately, to control. Additionally, if those messages were given by the very people you looked to for love and guidance, the very ones whose opinions you trusted, they have been given the appearance of validity and have added weight.

Just as this book will help you identify the abuse, it will also help you identify the abuser. Emotional abusers have very select ways they use to control those they are abusing. The tragedy is that while often these abusers are aware of what they are doing, often they are not. A habit of abuse has become a life pattern that is so comfortable, so normal for them, they've stopped questioning the reasons behind their words and actions. As is so often the case in abuse, the abusers often have a history of abuse in their own past and are acting out behavior that seems normal to them.

Remember as you're reading this book, it is important to avoid trying to measure your abuse against some scale. Whether it is a long-term abusive relationship or a onetime traumatic event of rejection that created a later resentment and unresolved anger, it is still damaging. It is vital that you identify it and learn how to deal with its consequences. Acknowledging and becoming aware of abusive patterns in your life will lead to healing and the recovery process.

2

Why Is
Emotional Abuse
So Common?

There's an often-told parable about a man who goes to work. He arrives, only to find that his boss is fuming, running around the office screaming because the central office called and complained about a missed production schedule. The man gets chewed out by his boss all day for a variety of reasons. Upon finally arriving home after being verbally beaten all day, he finds that his wife has spent too much time shopping and dinner isn't on the table yet. Erupting in anger at his wife, he storms off to watch television until dinner. His wife then turns around and immediately unloads on their son for leaving his shoes in the middle of the floor. The boy gets mad and kicks the cat.

We've Learned to Ignore It

Emotional abuse is like the parable—pervasive, self-perpetuating, and so common everyone can relate to it. In fact, that's part of the problem: It is so common. Being a part of the cultural, social, and personal landscape, it has come to be ignored. As long as anyone can remember, Grampa talked that way to Dad, who talked that way to Junior, who in turn talks that way to his own kids.

It probably seemed as if it wasn't just your family. The neighbors down the street could often be heard yelling at their kids in the summer when the windows were left open. The kids on the street would escape their houses, meet somewhere, and swap horror stories about their parents.

Perhaps that's how you grew up, thinking adults always dealt with kids that way. So you learned to survive the yelling matches and duck when the blows came. Or you just left and got out of the way. Whoever said life was fair, anyway? Tragically, more often than not, even though you hated the way you'd been treated, you found yourself doing the same thing with your own kids, especially when you were stressed out or tired.

As you were growing up, the sarcastic remarks, negative messages, and disrespect shown you may have seemed part and parcel of your relationship with others in your family. It was just the way everyone spoke to each other. You thought you'd learned to deal with it, to let it roll off your back and not bother you. All of the evidence you could see seemed to indicate that the way you were treated was normal. It might not have felt good, but that was normal too.

Even turning on the television bolstered this image that your life was normal. For those old enough to remember, the show *The Honeymooners* in its heyday gave weekly examples of verbal put-downs and sarcastic remarks. Later *All in the Family* would parody the wisecracking, ill-tempered Archie constantly putting down his wife, his daughter and son-in-law, his coworkers, and his neighbors. Even in this "enlightened" day and age, the use of verbal put-downs and sarcasm is still used to provoke laughter. In the cartoon show *The Simpsons*, the father is portrayed as a bad-tempered man constantly yelling at his sarcastic, wisecracking kid, who in

turn takes great pride in his ability to outsmart authority figures, and who constantly lives down to his father's poor
expectations. Homer spends each week reminding Bart fre-
quently and loudly just what he thinks of him.

Even if we consider ourselves enlightened, we sometimes
find ourselves laughing at this abusive treatment. Why do we
laugh? Because the abuse makes us tense up inside; laughter
releases some of the tension. We can watch from the side-
lines, in control, and experience the release and relief because
we are not the victims.

Like a constant ringing in the ears or background noise,
the frequency of emotional abuse has caused us to seek to
ignore it since we can't seem to ever get away from it. And
if we can ignore it, we can deny not only its existence but
also its effects.

We've Learned to Deny It

Connie was forty-three years old and miserable. She didn't
have any energy and was depressed all of the time. Her life
seemed to be one long black tunnel. She thought it was
because her children had grown up and left home. She kept
telling herself she just didn't have enough to do anymore to
keep busy. Married young, she'd never held a "real" job,
instead she stayed at home and raised her children. After the
last child moved out, she had occupied herself at first by com-
pulsively cleaning the house and using up her days in little
projects. But lately even that was becoming pointless. The
energy to keep up an empty house had dissipated, along with
her joy.

Some of her friends urged Connie to go out and get a job
or volunteer her time at a library, school, or hospital. But
Connie was convinced she could never handle a "real" job
since she'd always stayed home. Her husband's reaction to
that suggestion had been immediate—she had no skills, and
who would want a fat, middle-aged woman for *anything*?

Besides, lately she couldn't even do her housework or have a hot meal on the table when he got home. He was really afraid for her. If she did get a job, he knew she'd be fired in no time at all.

At first her husband's words had hurt Connie's feelings, but deep down she knew he was right. He was just trying to save her from the embarrassment of failure. All the time growing up she'd heard how she was stupid and slow, that all she'd ever be good for was having babies. She knew then that her parents hadn't really meant to hurt her; they were just trying to save her from having unreal expectations about what she could do with her life.

And they'd been right. She'd never been any good at anything except raising her kids. That was the only thing she'd ever done right, the only thing she could take any pride in, and now they were gone.

Finally, Connie had sunk so low she sought help for her depression. If someone could only help her figure out what to do with the rest of her life, she'd be happy and able to function again. But instead of looking at what to do with her future, Connie was guided by her therapist into looking at her past. For every example, past or present, that she could think of where she'd been emotionally abused, Connie was able to come up with a perfectly good reason to deny the negative and destructive nature of those messages, to excuse the abuse and, by extension, the abuser. After all, those who had been the most abusive to her had also been those she loved.

Since childhood she'd denied the truth about herself. She'd denied the truth about her parents and how they treated her. She'd even denied the truth that her children had always been more important to her than her husband. To her children she was something, but to her husband she was nothing. In order for Connie to truly get on with her life, she had to rethink her pattern of denial and recognize that what she'd experienced as a child and as a wife was wrong, even if everything she'd ever learned said otherwise.

Central to this ability to outwardly ignore emotional abuse is the denial of its true nature and negative impact. Often two negative, abusive messages are passed on to children that reinforce the emotional abuse:

1. Whoever is in authority over you (be it parent, spouse, or boss) can speak to you however they see fit, no matter how negatively. Not only is it their right to address you as they desire, but it is probably for your own good.
2. "Sticks and stones may break your bones, but words can never hurt you."

These messages are delivered not only by power-hungry individuals bent on subjugating all those around them but also by everyday people who learned those messages themselves and never thought to question conventional wisdom.

Historically, the view has been taken that those who are strong or who hold a position of power are justified, because of that position or strength, in whatever action they choose to take against a weaker or subservient individual. Ancient conquerors took slaves of vanquished peoples as a matter of course. Feudal landowners dictated all aspects of the lives of their indentured peasants. Husbands could routinely beat their wives and children with impunity.

As civilization took hold and daily relationships came under scrutiny, oppressive behavior was identified and frowned upon. After World War II, the United States didn't enslave Germany or Japan—instead they were rehabilitated. Employers today have government-regulated standards in the workplace to protect workers. Men are now arrested for spousal abuse if they beat their wives and for child abuse if they beat their children.

While society has gone a long way toward making such outwardly aggressive behavior illegal, often it has turned a blind eye to the more subtle forms of oppression. While governmental and work relationships have been scrutinized, the family relationship has been considered private for most of this century. A man's house was his castle, and a man's family was his to rule as he saw fit as long as he didn't physically or sexually injure his wife or children. Parents were given a wide berth to treat their children as they desired. They were, after all, *their* children. It has only been in recent memory that women have stopped being thought of as property, and only within the last several decades that anyone has given thought to children as individuals separate from their parents.

As this new awareness has taken shape and behavior that was tolerated in times past becomes criminal, it has been the violent, the sexual, the obvious behavior that has been targeted for reappraisal. The woman who gets drunk and beats her child is now put in jail. But the same woman who gets drunk and spends an hour yelling at her child for trivial or imagined misbehavior is exercising her parental authority.

In addition, many cultures in the world today still hold the view that the dominant person in the relationship has the right to control that relationship. The husband is in charge of his wife. The mother is in charge of her children. The employer is in charge of the employee. The cultural acceptance of dominance in relationships allows for emotional abuse to take root. In most of these relationships there is a necessary component of authority that requires responsibility. But authority over a person has been twisted into dominion. To paraphrase an old axiom, "Absolute power corrupts absolutely and leads to abuse."

We've Learned to Accept It

It has only been recently that our inner-being, our emotional self, has been recognized and given value. In a physically demanding world, emotions were things for the weak, for women, for small children. Emotions were something you were supposed to grow out of. Emotional women were thought to be out of control. Stoicism was the preferred way to deal with the world. Straight-faced men and women were portrayed as strong, taking on the world and not letting it get to them. Little boys were taught not to cry or release their emotions as they got older. It was believed that part of the maturation process was learning to control one's emotions. Children were told they needed to be tough to get on in this world. Physical wounds by necessity would hurt, but the child was to steel himself so that harsh words would simply bounce off his toughened hide. "Sticks and stones may break my bones, but words can never hurt me," was the child's standard boast if another person verbally attacked him or her. Since this way of dealing with each other was so common, there was nothing special about being subjected to it. What was special was how well you could get beyond it, how well you could deal with it and not let it affect you.

You were taught to take the verbal attack head on, sluff it off, and go on with your life, throwing your indifference back into the faces of those who taunted you. Words weren't supposed to hurt you. If they did, there was something wrong with you. You had allowed someone else to gain the upper hand over you. You were weak, and therefore you deserved to be spoken to or treated in that way. In any case, if you were hurt, it was your fault.

Many of those I have worked with over the years learned to accept the world as it was given to them. They learned to accept relationships as they came to them. They looked around them and saw the same thing happening to others, so they accepted what happened to them as simply part of life.

Since the abuse is so normal growing up, people will often attempt to recreate that normalcy in future relationships. A man who has been verbally abused all of his life by his mother may, without thinking, be attracted to a woman who is loud and sarcastic. He doesn't see her behavior as strange or wrong. In fact, it will seem quite normal to him. He accepted the abuse as a child and continues to accept it from his wife as an adult.

We've Learned to Perpetuate It

Bill and his wife, Margaret, brought in their teenage son, Kevin, who was becoming increasingly rebellious and hard to control. He was throwing things around in his room, staying out late with friends whom Bill did not accept, and coming home drunk. After running out of options, and on the advice of their son's school, they sought professional help to sort out their differences.

Bill was convinced that a therapist would tell Kevin to clean up his act, learn to behave responsibly as a near-adult, and stop engaging in his destructive, disobedient behavior of staying out late and partying. Bill believed that a professional would help Kevin jettison his childish behavior and learn to accept the realities of the adult world.

Bill thought the therapist would deal only with Kevin's behavior. He'd pretty much had it trying to talk to his son. It always seemed to end in both of them yelling at each other at the top of their lungs. Bill was determined to bring Kevin's behavior under control, and Kevin was just as determined not to be ruled by his father anymore. Bill was looking to the therapist to provide weight and a second opinion to his attempts to reason with Kevin. Bill had prepared himself for being told about all of the problems Kevin had. It would be hard, but these problems were a fact of their life. They had to be faced squarely and dealt with in an adult and responsible way.

Instead, Bill was challenged by Kevin's therapist to take a hard look at the way he was treating his son and the messages he was transferring to him. Bill had to turn his view around from the adult he expected Kevin to be to the child Kevin actually was.

Bill discovered that Kevin really did want to please him but felt he never could hit the mark. Frustrated after years of trying unsuccessfully, he had not only given up, but in anger he had rebelled against everything he knew his dad wanted him to be. Bill learned that the anger Kevin was feeling was brought on by a deep sense of loss that he could never gain his father's approval.

Kevin discovered that Bill really did love him—so much so that he wanted him to be perfect so that nothing bad would ever happen to him, and if it did, he would be tough enough to handle it. Kevin learned that Bill was raising him just the way Bill himself had been raised.

Bill realized how powerful his words and messages were in Kevin's life and how much Kevin needed positive, affirmative messages from his dad in order to grow and function. Bill learned it was okay to show Kevin his love, his fears, his hopes, his emotions. Kevin learned to begin to trust his dad.

As in other types of abuse, emotional abuse can be self-perpetuating. You accept the abuse, deny its impact, and ignore your inner-self so much that, if you're not alert and careful, you end up continuing the cycle within your own relationships. Either you again take up the role of the abused in your new relationship, or you switch roles and instead become the abuser.

Connie, the woman I wrote about earlier, perpetuated her abuse by initiating and continuing in a relationship with someone who reinforced the negative messages she had received as a child. Controlled as a child by her parents through the abuse, the thought of independence later in life was frightening and foreign.

Bill perpetuated his abuse by becoming the abuser, repeating the abusive patterns he'd learned as a child on his own son, seeking to control his son and his son's response to the world.

Ultimately, any abuse is about control, or the fear of losing control, and emotional abuse is no different. The abuser uses the abuse to take or keep control over the other person.

- The husband who constantly tells his wife she's stupid and can't do anything on her own is trying to keep his wife totally dependent on him, controlling the possibility that she might someday leave him.

- The mother who overshadows her daughter in all of her activities—picking out her friends, her clothes, her school—is trying to gain control over time by living through her daughter.

- The manager who stifles all creative thought at the plant, who issues endless instructions to his employees, who keeps a constant eye on all of the work in the office, is trying to control the possibility that someone beneath him might someday rise above him.

In each relationship, the abusers have learned techniques to control those underneath them and have no problem using those techniques to get what they need or think they need. People who have such a deep-seated need to control events and other people are really operating out of a terrible sense of insecurity and are afraid of life and spontaneity. The unpredictable is something to be feared and controlled. Often the most unpredictable thing in their life is the people around them, so they must be controlled at all costs.

Emotional abuse, while often the product of a person who has an obsessive need for control, can also come from people who are simply out of control. For whatever reason, they have given up trying to have order in their life, to discipline their words and behavior. They use their words and actions to vent all of their frustrations and anger at the world they see around them and the past they can't get beyond. Life as they see it has given them a raw deal. They're mad, and everyone's going to know it. As the old saying goes, "Misery loves company," and they're too tired or too defeated to keep their anger to themselves—so they vent it on whoever happens to get in their way. Tragically, often the reason for the anger and the bitterness comes from having been abused themselves.

Emotional abuse has been ignored, its effects have been denied, and its place within relationships accepted. The people doing the abuse may not even be aware of the harm they are inflicting on the other person. They assume that's the way it should be because that's the way they were brought up; there's nothing wrong with it. They assume that the control they are trying to exert over the other person is really for their own good.

Those who work with the inner-being of the individual know and understand how destructive those assumptions have been in the lives of people.

It's time we stopped ignoring the emotional abuse that goes on around us.

It's time we stopped denying that what we've experienced or practiced ourselves is really destructive behavior.

It's time we stopped accepting anyone being treated in an abusive manner, no matter who is doing it or to what degree it is taking place.

It's time we stopped perpetuating the abuse that has been so destructive to ourselves and our relationships.

3

Why Is Emotional Abuse So Damaging?

Robert is thirty-two years old. He has trouble holding a job for any length of time. He just seems to grate on people's nerves with his abrasive, blunt outbursts of displeasure at their behavior. Because of his inability to deal effectively with other people, Robert finds most of his employment success in jobs where he can work by himself. Unfortunately, while Robert works best alone, he also works slowly. He constantly second-guesses his own judgments on the job. Caught up in daydreams, he spends a good portion of his time imagining how people will respond to his work and what he will do and say in response. He wants to be ready for what he knows will come. Expecting and even anticipating a negative reaction, he seems to enjoy it since it vindicates what he's believed they were thinking all along. He's happy inside because he was right. To others, Robert comes across as defensive and hostile because he's already sure that any response to him will be negative.

Robert grew up as one of three children. Older than Robert, the other two couldn't relate to his childish behavior. Robert was raised with the indelible impression that his brother and sister were smarter, better looking, and bound to be more successful than Robert could ever hope to be. His parents loved him, but there was always the sense that Robert was an afterthought, that the real tradition of the family would be carried on by the older, more capable children.

In school, Robert was always teased by the other children who knew his brother and sister. He was a thin, unattractive child, whose dour expression set up a barrier without a word being spoken. Robert seemed to want to be left alone, and others were more than happy to oblige.

Robert grew up feeling that he would never amount to anything, that who he was as a person was not valued, and that people would always deal with him in a hostile manner. Anticipating their reaction, Robert sought to beat them to the punch by being openly hostile and abrasive in all of his relationships.

Even therapy was something to be met with a battle as far as Robert was concerned. He didn't like his therapist, didn't like her conclusions, and didn't like having to change the way he'd always dealt with the world. Robert didn't want to take the chance of being hurt. However, Robert absolutely didn't want to continue living the way he was.

His recovery will be slow, but as long as Robert listens to his inner-being, which softly whispers above the clamor of his self-doubt that he really is a good person, one day Robert will finally believe it.

Emotional abuse is so damaging because it outlives its own life span. Not only does it damage a person's self-esteem at the time it is done, it also sets up a life-pattern that daily assaults the inner-being. Present events and relationships are filtered through the negative messages and events of the past.

Behavior is unknowingly modified to produce results consistent with the established life-pattern. Through continued emotional assault, even a healthy life-pattern can be subverted by an abusive one.

Lack of Security

At the most basic level, emotional abuse robs you of your sense of security and value. In an attempt to bring order out of chaos, even the regularity of abuse can be substituted for a sense of what is normal.

One of the deepest needs of children is for consistency, including the certain knowledge that they are unconditionally accepted and valued by those who love them. Small children love the repetitive, constant nature of certain stories, where the same words or phrases are used over and over again. Children learn what to expect, anticipate with delight the coming use of the word or phrase, and feel in control of the story when they can repeat along with the storyteller the right words at the right time. Toddlers will often ask for the same book to be read over and over again, until their parents are so sick of it they could just scream!

What can be boring to adult minds can be very comforting and affirming to children. The story always ends the same way. Life has order. By knowing the ending in advance, children have a sense of security and safety. They learn how it feels to be right, to know what lies ahead, and this produces a sense of control.

With emotional abuse, whether through purposeful or unknowing neglect, children soon learn that anything is possible. They never know the ending in advance. There are no boundaries for behavior directed toward them or attitudes thrust upon them.

Where there are no boundaries, there is no security. An interesting study of school children was conducted concerning their reaction to physical boundaries in their school playground. It found that when a fence was present in their school yard, they happily played right up to its crisscrossed edges. They knew where the boundary of their world was and took advantage of every inch; it allowed them to relax and play in safety.

When the fence was removed, the children huddled together close to the school building and did not venture down the hill to where the fence had been. Without the fence, they did not have a clear sense of boundary, of security. Instead of the removal of the fence promoting greater freedom, it produced heightened anxiety and unpredictable behavior. The presence of the boundary brought freedom. Removal of the boundary brought fear.

When a child lives in a household where there are no boundaries on adult behavior, fear is the immediate result. Never safe, never secure, the child learns to expect and anticipate the sudden, the violent. A blow can come at any time, be it physical or verbal. Accomplishments can be met with apathy, passive-aggressive indifference, or outright aggressive disapproval. It is best to be left unnoticed. It's safer that way.

Fear

A loss of security leads to an ever-present feeling of anxiety or fear. When you are in the midst of being emotionally abused, there is a very real fear of how far the abuse will go and how damaging it will be. You cringe and hope against hope that it won't go on as long as last time, or at least it won't be any worse.

You learn there are no safe moments. Your abuser may be absent, but he or she can reappear at any time. What met with an apathetic response yesterday may meet with violent outrage tomorrow. You are robbed of the security of anticipation. Unlike the child who knows the right words that come at the right time in the story, for the abused child there are no right words, and there never seems to be a right time.

Besides, the storyteller never tells the ending the same way twice. There is no order, no sense to be made from the events swirling around you. There is only the fear of what each day will hold.

The human mind has a fascinating need to form order out of chaos. Visually you have an ability called *closure*. If you look at a picture where some of the lines and details are missing, your mind fills in the blank, and you actually think you have seen the whole picture. You haven't; you've just seen parts. But your mind fills in the rest so completely you can visually be fooled into thinking you see what actually isn't there.

In the same way, your emotional makeup strives to produce closure on the bits and pieces of what happens to you. When you don't know why things happen, you fill in the blanks. The oppressive anxiety and fear you feel must have a reason. What is happening to you must have a reason. Too often your abuser is ready to supply you with one. Not the right one, but you don't have the capacity to know that. A reason is provided for the abuse, and you accept it.

Guilt

The reason that is provided for the abuse varies: You are bad, or stupid, or ugly, or unwanted, or the wrong sex, or the wrong age, or the wrong blood. Whatever the reason provided, you are to blame for what is happening to you. You are guilty of causing the abuse.

The guilt you are feeling is not true guilt. True guilt is brought on by a realistic understanding of your behavior and its consequences to yourself and others. False guilt is that oppressive burden that is not based on reality but on the warped views, ideas, and attitudes of others. Emotional abuse transfers those warped views onto yourself.

For some, assuming the guilt for the abuse might seem to be a devastating decision—and it is—but it also has some very practical uses. For the person who has been emotionally abused, guilt is born out of a sense of fear of the world and what it holds. At first it makes no sense that this should be happening, but then guilt takes over. You feel responsible. You are told you are responsible. Some of the nameless chaos is encapsulated. *Bad things happen to me because I am bad.* A sense of order is established. By latching onto your guilt, you are really attempting to take back control over your life.

If I am guilty of causing the bad things that are happening to me, then all I have to do is change my behavior, my looks, my weight, to stop causing the bad things. To children, this is a very logical conclusion. It is a way of asserting that they really do have some control over the way they are being treated.

At first children who are abused in this way will attempt to so completely control their behavior that they do nothing that angers their abuser. They will often appear to be model children—compliant, quiescent, acting extremely adult. They are praised by other adults for their behavior. They begin to hope that they have found the key that will stop the abuse. Hand in hand with false guilt is false hope. Hope that if they are just good enough, thin enough, bright enough, hard-working enough, the abuse will stop, and the people who are supposed to love them will finally start acting loving. By accepting the mantle of guilt, the child expects a payoff in hope. *If I can just be lovable, surely then you will love me.*

Just as your eyes deceive you with closure, your heart can deceive you with false guilt. You can so completely see the proof of your own guilt that it affects the very mental image of yourself that you carry around inside. You are guilty. You are bad. You deserve the awful things that happen to you, that people say to you. Something is wrong with the world if you are not punished. The overwhelming feeling of guilt becomes what is normal. If others do not punish you, you will punish yourself so that order may be maintained. You will desire to create what you were used to enduring and used to feeling. In essence: Better the hell you know than the heaven you do not.

Tragically, the abused child accepts guilt to buy hope, hope that he or she can control the situation. The human heart has a tremendous capacity to hope. This is especially true of the heart of a child because there is still plenty of room for hope to stretch its edges. The scarring of disappointment hasn't started to restrict and bind.

As year after year of disappointment builds, as time after time the abuse has continued no matter what the abused child has done to control his or her behavior, the abused heart will begin to harden. Hope can no longer find a suitable home. Disappointment leads to frustration and anger, which results in resentment slowly creeping in.

> *I'll never be good enough.*
> *Mom will never like the way I look.*
> *I'm too fat for anyone to ever love me.*
> *I'll never be smart enough to get a real job.*
> *I guess Dad was right when he said I'd end up on the streets.*

Hope hasn't worked. It was false all along. Controlling your own behavior hasn't worked. The abuse continues. Disappointment and resentment must now be contended with. But they rarely come alone.

Anger

When security is gone, when fear must be dealt with on a daily basis, when the oppressive weight of guilt crushes the spirit, when hope is extinguished in the rush of despair, often the only way to respond is with anger. The injustice of the abuse eventually demands the response of rage from the battered psyche of the abused person.

This rage and anger is explosive and consuming. It can take opposite directions in its release. In the abused person, often this anger is directed inward. Presented daily with "proof" of total unworthiness, the emotionally abused can turn the frustration on themselves. In my practice I have seen children who habitually injure themselves. They will hit their heads repetitively on a wall, with almost hypnotic ferocity. Their frustration and anger, having no other outlet, is released on their own bodies. The pain they feel becomes a kind of purging of their all-consuming anger.

For bulimics the very act of purging either by vomiting or laxatives is a violent rejection of their own bodies. I have also worked with bulimics who release their anger by secretly cutting themselves with razor blades on their arms and legs.

It is said that depression is only anger turned inward. Emotionally abused people often give up on emotions, since emotions have proven to be so damaging. They have been beaten down by the emotions of others and struck through the heart by their own emotions in response. No safety, just anger, fear, and guilt. *Perhaps*, they think, *if I punish myself there will be no need to be punished by others.* Or, *I'm only getting what I really deserve.*

This resulting anger can take another route to expression in the emotionally abused. When they have finally had enough, they can vent their own anger and aggression on the person who has abused them. In today's society there is a legal condition being used as a defense in murder and injury trials known as "the battered woman syndrome." It depicts a woman who has been so emotionally, physically, and/or sexually abused by a lover or spouse that the only way she can see to remove herself from the situation is to actually kill her abuser. In a violent, uncontrollable act of rage, she attempts to reestablish control over her life by killing the man who has been controlling her through his abuse.

This dramatic act is not the norm, however, for those who have been abused. More often I have found the anger directed inward, or if the anger is directed outward, it most often is not directed at the person who caused the abuse. Often that person is absent from the abused adult's life, either by distance or by death. Usually the abused has continued the life-pattern by maintaining relationships with an abuser of some kind. The anger is then transferred to a different relationship, a spouse, parent, or even a coworker. Wherever it is transferred, the results are the same—a desperate attempt to control or influence others in improper ways such as passive-aggressive manipulation or a domineering attitude.

However it is manifested, for those who are abused there is a tremendous feeling of rage. For the most part it is kept tightly locked away, out of sight. To let it escape would mean to face the rancid reality of failed hope. So it stays tightly controlled, year after year, hidden, bound, while the rest of the personality makes the transition from child to adult.

A lack of security brings about fear, which brings about guilt, which perpetuates false hope, which results in anger. Fear, guilt, and anger—three of our most powerful emotions. Emotional abuse is so damaging because of the way it sets you up to deal with these three powerful emotions.

Fear, guilt, and anger are not negative emotions. Emotions, in and of themselves, are not good or bad, positive or negative. They are simply involuntary reactions to the world around us. The positive and negative (or good and bad) labels result from what we've learned to do to deal with our natural emotions.

Fear prompts a child not to put her hand on a hot burner. Instead of being negative, fear has kept her from serious injury.

Guilt over hitting another child prompts genuine remorse and a desire to control emotions in the future. True guilt, instead of being negative, is helping to mold future appropriate behavior.

Anger at seeing an injustice take place has often motivated someone to change the course of history by his or her response. Far from being negative, anger has provided the fuel to keep going in the face of adversity.

In order to mature into healthy, well-adjusted adults, all children must learn how to deal effectively with the fear, guilt, and anger they feel. These are powerful emotions, which can be used for much learning and good when harnessed properly. It is hard enough in normal households to learn how to react to these emotions wisely. All of us, if we are honest, could probably admit that we are still learning how to deal with our fear, guilt, and anger.

Someone who has been emotionally abused is left to feel all of these emotions—not only those that have been produced appropriately, but also those that have been produced inappropriately by the abuse they have suffered—without the adult guidance and help to put them into perspective.

- How can a child go to an adult for help with an unnatural fear when the very thought of how that adult might react produces an even greater fear?
- How can a child reach out for forgiveness and perspective in dealing with guilt when all she has been told up to this point is how worthless she is?
- How can a child receive love and forgiveness for reacting in rage and anger when the response of choice from the adult is a verbal tongue-lashing?

Not only are emotionally abused children left to come to grips with these emotions themselves, they are also overloaded with anger, fear, and guilt through the actions of the adults around them. Not only do they not see the proper response to these emotions modeled by those around them, they also see the improper response put forward as the example they are to follow.

People who were emotionally abused as children have a real problem dealing with fear, guilt, and anger as adults. Their childhoods have been damaged by the abuse they've suffered, and their adult lives have been sabotaged as well. Emotional abuse is particularly damaging because of this continuing effect. The best way for an abused adult to be healed is to go back and deal with the abused child inside to help him or her come to grips with the overwhelming feelings of fear, guilt, and anger. You can make a decision as an adult to learn healthy ways of dealing with your anger, fear, and guilt!

Part Two

Types
of
Emotional
Abuse

4

Emotional Abuse through Words

Words can be powerful tools or powerful weapons. The weapon of choice for emotional abusers is often verbal. They use their words to wound, to entrap, to imprison. Through their words and tone of voice, they imprint messages on the minds of those who hear. These messages, repeated often and forcefully, infiltrate through to the inner-being of the victims, shaping the way they view themselves.

While each person is different, there are several distinct ways the emotional abuser can use to dispense his or her abuse. It may be a single form or a combination of forms, however, most are recognizable. As you read through this chapter, think back over people you have known. You probably will be able to come up with at least one name for every type of abuse.

The Overbearing Opinion

Carrie hated going shopping with her mother. If she wanted to go to Penney's, her mother insisted they travel to Sears. If she chose a pink sweater to try on, her mother would loudly proclaim that blue was a *much* better color on her, and besides a blouse was much more practical than a sweater.

If Carrie started dating Kevin, her mother would manage to mention three or four times how much more suitable Mark was. She had a thousand reasons why Kevin just didn't quite come up to her high standards.

Before Carrie left for school, she prayed her mother would be preoccupied and wouldn't notice what she was wearing, how much makeup she had on, what time she was leaving, or whom she was planning to meet after school. Carrie's mother had an opinion about *everything*. It never seemed to correspond with what Carrie was thinking.

All of her life, Carrie moved within the shadow of her mother's opinions. There was never anything insignificant enough for her mother to be neutral about. From the temperature of the room to the volume of the television to the position of the chair, Carrie's mother altered her surroundings to fit her preferences. Other people were simply not consulted.

As a child, Carrie soon learned that it did no good to argue or attempt to explain her own opinions to her mother. Carrie felt her mother just wasn't interested in what she thought. Depending on her mother's mood, confronting her could bring disastrous consequences to Carrie's life. It simply wasn't worth the risk, not for Carrie or anyone else in the family for that matter.

Resigned to always keep her opinion to herself, Carrie discovered as an adult she had a hard time making decisions. Distrusting her own opinions, she would often look to someone else, a dominant personality, to validate her own thoughts and decisions. As a child Carrie had learned she wasn't a competent judge.

I once saw a sign that read, "Everyone is entitled to their own opinion, as long as it agrees with mine!" This is the essence of the overbearing opinion. The sign I saw was in jest, but for the emotional abuser, this is a life-statement. It defines how he or she views the world and everyone else in it.

Healthy discussion, on the other hand, allows for the expression of a variety of opinions on any given subject. Few things can be said to be black or white in reality. Most opinions are very personal and are derived through experiences, knowledge, and personal preferences. Because individuals are unique, the opinions they arrive at will necessarily be different. This brings variety, contrast, and flexibility, all of which enhance healthy relationships.

We communicate through facts, opinions, and feelings. Facts are just that—indisputable segments of reality. "The sun is out, the sky is blue, and the birds are singing," could be facts about a day in the park.

We also communicate through opinions. "It certainly is crowded here today," or, "This is the best park in the city for taking a walk," are opinions based on experiences, knowledge, and personal preference.

Finally, there are feelings. "It makes me happy to see the ducks swim in the pond," and, "I love to walk in the grass without my shoes on," are statements of feelings.

Statements of fact, the first example, rarely come under dispute. But opinions and feelings, the second and third examples, are subjective observations. They are personal perspectives on the day in the park.

The abuser with the overbearing opinion restricts the flow of free expression, treating his or her opinions and feelings as if they were as incontrovertible as facts. This robs the recipient of the experience of trial and error, of exploring his or her own thoughts, likes, and dislikes. It superimposes the personality of the abuser onto the abused, stifling the ability to bloom on his or her own.

Healthy give and take in relationships allow for an honest, gentle exchange of feelings and opinions. However, when opinions or feelings are forced on us, we resist and often rebel. Not only are we not allowed to have our own thoughts, we are forced to accept unfamiliar ones.

The Person Who Is Always Right

Mike cringed inside. He stood waiting for the words he had heard so often in his life. "I told you so," said his father with a tight lip. His dad was furious, and Mike set his jaw, clenching his teeth. It would only be worse if he blurted out what he so wanted to say: "You're always right! You're never wrong about anything!" Once, just once, Mike wished he could prove his father wrong.

His father had told him the car wasn't in good shape when he'd bought it, but Mike really didn't care at the time. He just wanted the car. Sometime, halfway into his dad's lecture, Mike had just tuned him out. Somewhere between the explanation of the fuel system problems and the bald tires, Mike had stopped listening and started hoping. Hoping this time his dad would be wrong.

Now he had to admit it, his father had been right about the fuel pump, though he really hadn't listened to what Mike was trying to tell him. Mike knew the car wasn't perfect, but it was a good deal anyway. It might not have been the car his father would have chosen, but Mike was still happy with his choice, fuel system and all. No matter what Mike tried to say, his dad wouldn't listen. His dad was right about the car, and that was all there was to it.

Hand in glove with the overbearing opinion abuser is the person who is always right. The overbearing-opinion abusers have an idea or opinion about everything. The person-who-is-always-right abusers do not make the same volume of pronouncements, but when they do, they always position themselves in the right and everyone else in the wrong. They will sift through events and information for proof of their rightness, bombarding anyone who questions them with a list of reasons why they are correct in their thinking. There is no room for a second opinion.

Neutral in circumstances in which they have no interest, these abusers are tenacious whenever they feel compelled to render a decision. *What* is right is not the important thing as much as the *fact* of their rightness. Even when normal people would admit their error, abusers who are always right will find a way to justify their decision. If it cannot be justified by the circumstance, they will often manufacture a plausible reason. In other words, even if the event turned out wrong, they were still right.

Unlike the overbearing opinion, the person who is always right allows other people to have differing opinions. If the other person is shown to be right, that is often met with a studied indifference—as if it wasn't that big a deal in the first place. However, if the other person is wrong, the failure is pointed out strongly and loudly.

Living with a person who is always right produces frustration and anger. Events are constantly being turned around in his or her favor. You begin to think there is no justice in the world, since your abuser never has to admit his or her error. More importantly, you may also begin to believe that your abuser has been right all along. Like living with the overbearing opinion, you begin to second-guess your ability to make decisions, for they never seem to be the right ones.

Realistically, no one is always right or always wrong. All of us are plenty of both. In healthy relationships, forgiveness is extended when wrong, and graciousness shown when right.

The Judge and Jury

Darlene was sixteen years old. She entered therapy through a court-ordered decision. After she was caught shoplifting at a local department store, the judge had decided to see if family counseling might alter Darlene's classic path toward juvenile delinquency. She hadn't wanted to come, but Darlene was quite used to absolute decisions and pronouncements.

Darlene's father was the unwavering decision-maker in the family. It didn't matter what anyone else decided, everything was dependent on whatever ruling her father laid down. The whole family could have planned something as simple as a night out for dinner. But if Father decided he was too tired, they all stayed home. If Mother had said it was all right for Darlene to spend the night at a friend's house, but Father didn't want her to be gone, she just couldn't go. No arguments, no amount of persuading could change his mind once it was set. His decisions were final. No appeals process. Verdict reached and decision rendered.

Darlene soon learned that his decisions usually had very little to do with the circumstances and very much to do with how he was feeling at the time. If he was in a good mood, he could be generous. If he was in a bad mood, all bets were off. There was no reliable standard, only convenience or inconvenience, for her father's decisions seemed to be based most often on what it meant to him. If he had to drive her anywhere, forget it. If it meant he had to leave the house after he got home, forget it.

Darlene learned to filter all her decisions through the what's-in-it-for-me lens. She learned not to consult anyone else about what she had decided to do. Consequently, some of Darlene's choices were inappropriate ones. During therapy she was able to see that her father's model of making decisions was flawed.

All of us can probably think of a person who acts as if he or she is the sole judge and jury for making decisions. Akin to the person who is always right, the judge-and-jury abusers allow no opposition to their will.

But the judge-and-jury abusers not only make the decisions, they also make the laws. What might be reason for doing something on Monday may cease to be a reason on

Tuesday. It doesn't matter if a decision is right, as long as it fills their needs in other ways. They are not so concerned with the process of the decision, like the person who is always right, as they are the outcome of the decision—which is to have happen what they want done.

The right or wrong of what they decide is irrelevant. To the judge-and-jury abusers, the most important thing is their position, to be in control of the people around them. It is their call to make, whether good or bad. Others are to obey them, not because they have rendered a good decision, but because they are the authority.

In healthy parent-child relationships, children have to learn to obey their parents' decisions, often without total understanding of why those decisions are made. Small children learn that adults are authority figures who need to be obeyed. A toddler shouldn't stop to question an adult decision that he get out of the street. Such obedience can be very important for the safety of the child, especially if a car is traveling in his direction.

However, the judge-and-jury abusers use the obedience of others not for good or safety, but for their own comfort or control.

The power to demand obedience is a great responsibility. When we obey others, we submit to their will above our own. Therefore, this power should be used sparingly and only with the other person's best interests in mind. Power should never be misused for personal comfort, gain, or control.

The Put-Down Artist

"So, you really think you can get that job, huh? What a joke! Why in the world would anyone want to hire you?" Jeff's older brother sneered at him with disgust.

"Well, I guess 'cause I'm a hard worker, and I'm willing to learn," Jeff responded angrily, feeling that familiar knot tying up in his stomach.

"Hard worker? Right. If you're such a hard worker, how come you don't get better grades?"

Jeff felt like he'd been hit in the stomach this time. "My grades aren't that bad. I do the best I can!"

"I'll let you in on a little secret, kid," Dennis got up right next to him, put his arm around his shoulder, and whispered loudly, "Your best isn't all that great!"

"Maybe not," Jeff replied, twisting out of his brother's arm, "but I'm trying for that job anyway!"

"Perfect!" Dennis exclaimed, throwing himself back down on the couch and turning up the sound on the stereo. "Now all my friends can go see my little brother wearing a dweeb hat, bagging fries at Mac's. 'May I take your order, sir?' What a joke! . . . Hey, kid," he yelled, as Jeff left the room muttering under his breath. "Try not to fall into the fryers!"

Emotional abuse can come from different sources in a variety of ways. Some of the most destructive abusers are people who habitually put down another person through their words. Instead of using their speech to encourage and lift up the other person, they use it to crush and to discourage. Their use of language and their tone of voice is chosen purposely to degrade the feelings of the other person, to make them feel valueless. It is almost as if their words become a verbal heel grinding down the self-esteem of the abused.

There is nothing veiled or subtle about this form of abuse. It connects with the intensity of a right hook to the jaw. There is never any doubt how these abusers really feel about their victims. Their speech is littered with verbal garbage spewed directly at the abused. It does no good to duck. It will always find its mark.

Put-down artists attempt to bring themselves up by pushing everyone else down. Usually their degree of self-contempt is evident in the intensity with which they degrade others. Whatever the reason for the abuse, its effects are still the same for the abused. Life becomes a verbal minefield where

anything you say can and will be used against you . . . at any
time . . . for any reason.

If you are a victim of a put-down artist, you learn to suspect all relationships. A casual word, a thoughtless remark by
anyone else, is immediately taken as a personal insult, a mad-
dening slight on your personhood. The result for the abused
is suspicion and hostility in dealing with other people. There
are no comfortable, relaxed relationships. There is no humor.
Everything is taken literally and negatively. This form of emotional abuse is the verbal equivalent of physical beating, and
the most likely form to be accompanied by it.

All of us have spoken something in anger that was meant
to hurt someone else. But in healthy relationships, those
instances should be rare. Even when those angry words come,
there is a deposit of good words and healthy interaction to
draw on so the rash remark can be put into proper perspective, apologized for, and forgiven.

The Stand-Up Comic

"Jane's such an airhead, it's a wonder she doesn't float
away completely!"

"Did you hear what Bob over in engineering did to his car
the other day? He was so busy working out his gas mileage,
he ran out of gas!"

"Like Shirley really deserved that raise! Like she's so hard-
working! The only thing she ever worked hard for around
here is making the most of her coffee breaks!"

"What a moron Joe down in the garage is! The only way
he's gonna move up in the world is to climb on top of a car!"

The stand-up comic is just that—only the butt of his jokes
is always you. You're his eternal straight man. He doesn't
laugh *with* you, he laughs *at* you. Through sarcasm and exag-
geration, he beats down your self-image.

Very similar to the put-down artist, the stand-up comic
instead uses a twisted humor. Where the put-down artist

makes use of a club, the stand-up comic uses a whoopee cushion. The jokes are often in public where his or her humor encourages others to participate in your abuse. After all, it's just a joke, and the stand-up comic is very clever at finding what is considered funny in any given situation.

Everyone seems to be laughing, so how come you don't think it's funny? Because the humor is being gained at your expense. The humiliation you feel is the fuel for the sarcasm and the jokes. Your shame energizes your abuser.

This kind of abuse provides a way out, an instant excuse for any injury caused. After all, if you're the only one who isn't laughing, there must be something wrong with you. Everyone else seems to be able to take a joke, so why can't you?

This type of abuse can leave a deep sense of outrage at being used for another person's pleasure. The abuser gets all the laughs, and you are left to feel humiliated and small inside. Often the only defense against this type of abuse is to become a clown yourself, beating your abuser to the punch by beating up on yourself. Better to be the class clown than the verbal punching bag.

While it is important to a healthy self-image to be able to laugh at ourselves and our foibles, it is not healthy to allow yourself to be used as the punch line for other people's jokes. There's nothing funny about the way it makes you feel.

The Great Guilt-Giver

I first met Renee when she came, reluctantly, into my clinic. She couldn't have weighed more than eighty pounds. Her face was skeletal, skin drawn back over protruding cheekbones on a body made pencil-thin by forced starvation. Even in her condition, Renee was convinced she was hideously fat.

It didn't take long for me to uncover why Renee was trying to destroy herself. Renee was living under the burden of tremendous guilt. After all, if it hadn't been for her mother becoming pregnant with Renee, her mother might have gone on to become one of the premier dancers in a prestigious dance company on the East Coast. If Renee's mother hadn't put on fifty pounds while pregnant with Renee, she might have been able to get back into shape after giving birth. If it hadn't been for the fact that Renee's father had left soon after she was born, leaving Renee's mother to go to work full time, her mother might have had the time and energy to practice and find another dance company to work with. If it hadn't been for Renee, life might have been so much better for her mother.

So there was Renee: eighty pounds and trying desperately to be thin enough to fit the mold of a dancer. Eighty pounds and trying desperately to make up for all the damage she'd done to her mother's life. Eighty pounds and dying from the load of guilt dumped onto her by an unhappy, unfulfilled mother.

While the jokes of the stand-up comic can hit you all of a sudden like a ton of bricks, the weight of the guilt-giver comes on a brick at a time, just long enough for you to adjust to the weight before another one is added. Brick upon brick of guilt, year after year, message after message, remark after remark. Usually not delivered in haste or loudly, but with a sigh, with a sad, disappointed look that communicates you are the cause of all of his or her problems. If it weren't for you, life would be so much better.

If you were emotionally abused in this way you may feel as if you have no importance to your abuser. In fact, you may feel as if the abuser's life would be so much better if you weren't around to mess it up. Nothing could be farther from the truth.

For guilt-givers, the most important person in the world is the one on whom they heap their guilt. Without you, they would be responsible for their own failures. For whatever reason, life hasn't turned out like they wanted it to. But instead of being realistic about their goals and their own part in fulfilling them, they have chosen to shift responsibility from themselves onto you. The load of their own guilt is so crushing to them, they habitually shift some of it onto you. Faced with accepting themselves or harming you, they choose the latter.

Without you, there would be no one to draw recompense from. With you feeling guilty and at fault, there is always a way for you to "make it up" to the person you have "harmed." Maybe it's by never leaving them to form other relationships. Maybe it's always being there to do that errand, or pay that bill, or take care of whatever problem arises. After all, it really is your fault that they find themselves in such a mess in the first place. The least you can do is fix it for them.

Healthy guilt causes us to evaluate our actions and respond accordingly. Every one of us is guilty of some wrong behavior within a relationship. We're human—we make mistakes. True guilt is the response. It causes us to feel sorry for what we did, accept responsibility for the damage done, and do what we can to repair it.

Guilt-givers do not use true guilt. By manipulating the facts, they produce false guilt. The guilt is false because it is based on false information.

Renee was experiencing false guilt because her guilt was based on the "fact" that her birth ruined her mother's dancing career and thus her entire life. The truth both Renee and her mother needed to come to understand was that Renee's mother had made a choice to get married and leave her dancing career for her husband. When he left her, she was unable to return to the singular, devoted life of a dancer because she was caring for an infant. The real truth was that the decision to stop dancing was her mother's, not Renee's. Renee had had no say in the matter.

False guilt is slippery. Because it has no basis in truth, the reasons behind it can be altered by the abuser. If one reason stops working, another one can be substituted—whatever it takes to produce the desired guilt reaction. True guilt, on the other hand, can be met head-on, dealt with, worked through, and forgiven.

The Historian

Judy was ready for a fight. She'd come prepared. All her ammunition was stacked up and ready to be fired. The powder was primed and just looking for a spark to set it off. She'd had a bad day at work. She'd gained three pounds over the past week without eating *anything* wrong. Besides, she had the perfect excuse—her period was only a few days away. Tense and angry, she felt ripe to explode.

A couple of days earlier, her husband had made an offhand remark about a dress she had on looking a little tight. Granted, she'd asked him what he thought of it. Ever since, she'd been stewing about his answer.

When he walked in the door from working outside, she hit him full blast. "Get those muddy shoes off my clean carpet this minute!" Jumping back as if stung, her husband looked down at his footprints, barely visible on the rug.

"Aw come on, Judy, it's not so bad. Here, I'll take them off for you."

"You never care about the house! All the work I do around here you just take for granted!"

"No, I don't," he began to protest. "Besides, how many times do you compliment me on the yardwork?"

"I did two times last week. Once on Thursday morning on the way out to the car, and the other time was Sunday when you brought in the bouquet of flowers." Judy lobbed two shells in his vicinity. "When's the last time you said anything nice about the house, huh?"

"I always tell you how nice the house is!" her husband replied, confused.

"Oh, yeah? When was the last time?"

"I don't remember every single time I say something nice to you." Taking off the shoes was forgotten as her husband tried desperately to search for a bunker behind the kitchen counter.

Judy followed, relentless in her anger, sensing she was gaining the historical upper hand.

"Well I remember every mean thing you've said or done to me over the past ten years!" Shells arched across the kitchen tiles.

"You remember everything!" her husband fired back. "It doesn't matter how insignificant, or how much I said I was sorry, or how much you provoked me. I don't even remember saying or doing half of what you say I did!"

"Are you saying I'm lying?" Judy demanded, full of righteous indignation. Direct hit.

"No!" her husband protested, angry and confused.

It always seemed to turn out like this, every time they fought. He'd get so turned around he couldn't even remember why the argument started in the first place. All he could remember was the sickening feeling of dealing with Judy in one of her rages. He felt lost and out of his element. She'd bring up stuff he'd said years back. He couldn't remember why he'd said it, or if he'd even said it at all. Judy never seemed able to let go of the past. And her version of the past was always so much worse than he remembered.

Historians are a *This Is Your Life* nightmare. They are people who, like Judy, remember every bad thing you've ever done or they have thought you've done. With computer accuracy, all your bad moments are logged and recorded to be brought up in full detail at any future time the historians might deem appropriate. There is no getting beyond an event, no putting the past behind you and going forward. Like a heap of heavy luggage, historians drag all of it along with them.

The odd thing about historians is their view of the past is decidedly one-sided. They never seem to remember their own faults or mistakes with the same clarity they recall yours. If you bring up one event in your defense, they can come up with a multitude of others to bury it in a verbal barrage.

This type of emotional abuse is dangerous because the historians seem to be presenting facts. They back up those facts with details: dates, places, actual conversations. It is easy to become overwhelmed with the information and give in to the demands of the abuser. But often the facts being presented are instead the abuser's opinion of what you said and why. A word, a phrase, an intonation can be changed to produce a completely different intent than the one you had when you said it. It isn't so much *history* as it is *historical fiction*, based on the truth, but altered for dramatic content.

In healthy relationships, the positive and happy memories are those that survive. The others are dealt with and forgiven, and the relationship is allowed to continue on. Each of us makes mistakes on a daily basis. If these mistakes were merely piled up on top of each other, they would soon bury us. Historians can't forgive and forget, nor do they want to. Their manipulation of the past helps them to control people in their present and future.

Verbal abuse is like a tape recorder that never stops playing. On and on the messages run, over and over, year after year. You hear the words in your head whether you want to or not. They repeat themselves softly in the quiet moments when no one else is speaking. Like relentless waves undermining the sand, they steadily wash away the foundations of self-esteem and self-respect. Too often they become the background noise of our lives—too quiet to be really heard, too loud to be totally ignored.

As unpleasant as it may seem, the only way to deal with verbal abuse is to turn up the recorder. Really listen to what those messages are saying to you, find out when they were recorded and by whom, and begin to erase them by taping over them with positive, uplifting, encouraging messages of the self-esteem and self-worth that comes through healthy relationships.

5

Emotional Abuse through Actions

Emotional abuse can come not only through words but also through the actions that accompany those words such as physical intimidation, manipulation, and physical threats. Emotional abusers who use actions as well as words increase their arsenal of ways to manipulate and control. They attempt to control not only behavior, but circumstances as well.

The Commander-in-Chief

Dennis Jones's father ran a tight ship. With military precision he controlled the lives of each member of the family. All had their assigned duties and responsibilities and were expected to carry them out with proficiency and efficiency. Slackers were not tolerated by Dennis's father, so Dennis made it a point never to be a slacker.

Life was a regimented routine at the Jones household from the time the children were awakened for school to the minute the lights were turned out at night. Of course exceptions needed to be made occasionally, but never regularly. Dennis's father liked order, and having other people participate in family decisions was messy. Dennis's mother went along with the program and backed up her husband in any dispute. The kids followed orders when they could and tried to cover up when they couldn't. Sometimes it worked; sometimes it didn't. Punishments were handed out with precision as well. So many whacks for each offense when they were younger. A designated length of time for a privilege to be withdrawn when they were older.

Life was carried out as expected—but there were rarely any surprises. There was consistency and order—but rarely any laughter or spontaneity. There was physical discipline—but rarely any physical affection. There was a sense of being part of a unit—but rarely of being a family.

Dennis couldn't wait to get out of the house.

Often emotional abusers will attempt to conceal the true purpose of their abuse—to control those around them. Commanders-in-chief, on the other hand, are completely open about what they are doing, if not why. They feel so comfortable in the role of controller, so confident in their ability to make the correct decisions for the people around them, so assured of their right of authority, that they openly direct the lives of others.

Unlike the judge and jury, whose reasons for making decisions often fluctuate according to circumstances or comfort, commanders-in-chief maintain a rigid code of behavior not only for others but also for themselves. Life is not something to be enjoyed but something to be controlled.

A relationship with this type of person is very difficult. It usually flows one way. Commanders-in-chief control the amount and type of interaction with others. While they may show their anger, they will rarely show their uncertainty. Their image as controller must be preserved at all times.

As the old *Mary Poppins* song goes, "A spoonful of sugar helps the medicine go down." It is so much easier to respond to authority when love and compassion accompany it. With the commander-in-chief, all you get is the bitter medicine.

Deprived of the affection and love you crave, you may rebel totally and live a life out of control, seeking comfort wherever you can find it. Or you may buy into the control and begin to pattern your own life as rigidly as you've been taught—rejecting any real need in your life for physical affection or closeness; not allowing other people in to disturb the orderliness of your life.

The healthy use of authority in any situation provides structure and order. It should also allow for the free flow of ideas and opinions from all concerned with a coordinated source of decision-making. When ideas and opinions are suppressed, emotional avenues are stopped up. Healthy authority creates structure. Unhealthy authority creates anger and frustration.

The Screamer

Jimmy's mom couldn't figure it out. All of a sudden her second grader didn't want to go to school anymore. Oh, he didn't just walk in the door and announce he was tired of school. Instead he started making up excuses why he just couldn't go. First his tummy hurt; then his head hurt; then his throat hurt; then he was too tired. Bright in class, Jimmy had always liked going to school, not only for what he could learn, but also to see his friends and play.

Finally his mom had had enough. Determined to get to the bottom of this, she began to question him about school.

"Why don't you want to go to school?" she asked him. He rolled his eyes trying to avoid hers. "Are any of the other kids giving you a bad time?"

"No, they're fine. . . . I just don't want to go . . . that's all." He was clearly uncomfortable talking to her.

"But you have to go to school, Jimmy. Besides, you're doing great! Mrs. Reed says you're one of her best students." At the name of his teacher, Jimmy became tense.

"I just don't want to," he pleaded.

"Is there something wrong with Mrs. Reed?" his mother asked, sensing her son's discomfort when she said the teacher's name.

"No," he said quickly. "She's my teacher."

"I know she's your teacher, but do you like her, Jimmy?"

"Well . . . she's a good teacher and all, but there is something I don't like about her," Jimmy admitted.

"What don't you like about Mrs. Reed?" His mother felt like she was pulling teeth, trying to be patient and give him the time he needed to tell her what was wrong, though warning signals were going off in her head.

"She screams all the time." There, he'd said it.

"I don't understand. What do you mean 'she screams all the time'?" His mother had been in class a few times and noticed his teacher had a tendency to raise her voice, but she assumed it was because she was nervous having a parent in the room. "I know when I've been in your class she's been a little loud, but there was a lot of talking going on."

"Mom," Jimmy said matter-of-factly, "it's ten times worse when you're not there. She yells at everyone, even if you're not doing anything wrong. If she even thinks you're doing something you shouldn't, she yells at you."

"I'm so sorry," she responded, taking her son in her arms. "Tomorrow I'll go to school and see the principal. What she's doing isn't right."

"Why does she yell so much, Mom?"

Most of us have had that unpleasant experience of being in the grocery store when a parent verbally unloads on a child. Usually she isn't even aware you're there, or else she doesn't care. Immediately you feel a rush of anger toward the parent and aching compassion for the child. Helpless, you watch and listen as the screamer vents her frustration on the cringing victim. But after the embarrassment is over, you can turn down the canned vegetables aisle and leave the unpleasantness behind you.

As hard as it is to hear such abuse, it is even more devastating to live with. The screamer is like a volcano who erupts in violent fits whenever the pressures of life get to be too much. As unpredictable as a real volcano, the screamer robs those around her of any sense of peace. It is the volatility of this type of abuser that produces an overwhelming fear of imminent disaster. Never safe, never secure—always on guard.

Anger or excitement causes our adrenaline to flow and increases the volume of our voice. It is the rush during a sporting event that causes us to enthusiastically yell at the top of our lungs. It is the scream of panic when danger presents itself. It is the snarl of anger when we are hurt or frightened.

For the screamer, the adrenaline flows all the time. The actions of others are constantly interpreted as threats, and the reaction is verbal rage. This flush of emotion can be very addictive. When rage is vented, the person feels powerful, invincible, in control. The bottled-up feelings are unleashed, releasing internal pressure. The release can be physically pleasurable, creating a desire to repeat it again and again.

As we have discussed before, anger is an emotion we all have. Depending on how we express it, anger can have positive or negative consequences. For screamers, anger is the emotion of choice. They are so filled with rage it seems to spill out whenever they open their mouths. But anger of this kind is seldom spent. It seems to have an inexhaustible core.

This type of abuse is most tragic when it occurs between parent and child. If you grew up in a household where you were constantly screamed at, in essence you were verbally attacked. Every time your abuser opened his or her mouth, you knew what was coming. Your stomach knotted up and your teeth clenched, preparing to withstand the onslaught. There was no use talking back or speaking up in your defense. That only made the attack worse, adding fuel to the fire. Better to shut up and take it. Better to stuff your own anger than add it to the mix. Anger will be expressed even in healthy relationships. People often do things that make us justifiably angry. But anger should never be an end in itself. Instead it should be a sign that something is wrong, that we've been hurt in some way, that something is left unresolved which needs to be dealt with so all concerned can go on.

The Intimidator

"If you don't play with me, I'll take my ball and go home."

"If you say one word to Mom or Dad, I'll tell them you were in on it."

"If you don't go to bed this instant, there'll be no television for a week!"

"If you don't play dolls with me, I'll tell Mom you hit me."

"If you don't go along with these figures for the audit, I'll make sure you don't have a job tomorrow."

"If you don't do what I want, I'll leave."

"If you . . . then I"—the classic words of intimidators. Their control over your behavior is always issued in the form of a threat. Sometimes it is delivered at the top of their lungs. Other times it can be slipped into the conversation on the wings of a whisper. However it is given, the threat is understood.

Intimidators can be of two types: the ones that are all talk with no real consequences behind their words, or the ones that mean every word they say and back it up with action. Either way, they present an unhealthy way of gaining whatever it is they desire.

Consequences are a fact of life. If I do A, then B happens. If I eat too many of the wrong foods, my body gets sick. If

I stay up too late at night, I'm tired in the morning. If I don't do my job correctly, I could be fired. But also, if I smile at someone, she may smile back. If I wake up in the morning deciding it's going to be a good day, it probably will be. If I do a good job at work, I'll most likely be appreciated. We all understand the role consequences play in our lives. The intimidator only knows the negative ones.

Each of us has a responsibility to those around us to explain what we need from them, how we feel about their actions, and what those actions mean to our lives. That's healthy. What is unhealthy is when those explanations become threats, when those explanations become battle lines drawn in the sand: "Step over this line and I'll deck you!"

Boundaries need to be set in any relationship. But boundaries should define the areas in which freedom can take place. Intimidators are not trying to set boundaries but to erect barriers, to keep you from doing anything they don't like.

Threats are most effective when they are actually carried out. If they are, the threatened person learns to deeply fear the intimidator. If they are not, the threatened person loses all respect for the intimidator, and the intimidator often feels compelled to up the ante, leading to escalating threats of harm or violence.

In healthy relationships, threats are not necessary. Trust and love provide the motivation for behavior.

The Roller Coaster

"Whose turn is it?" the oldest one asked. It was always her job to ask.

"It's not mine!" the youngest said quickly, shaking her head, eyes wide.

"It must be me," the middle child acknowledged reluctantly. "As soon as I know, I'll come back up and tell you."

"Okay," the oldest said, patting him on the shoulder. "Just make it seem normal."

"I know. I know." With that, he started down the stairs toward the kitchen. Mom was up, and it was his job to find out what sort of mood she was in. If she was in a good mood, he'd know it pretty quickly, and he would run back upstairs to his sisters and let them know they could relax for a while. If she was in a bad mood, it might take a little longer to show up, but sooner or later he'd catch it for something. Then as soon as he could, he'd go upstairs and prepare the others for the rest of the day. A good mood meant they could relax. A bad mood meant do everything you're told, don't argue, and above all don't get in her way!

They rotated the duty every weekend. During the week there was school and everything was rushed, so even if she was in a bad mood, they'd be at school soon. If she was in a good mood, there was no telling if it would last until they got home. With all the activities after school, it was every man for himself then. But on the weekend, it was important to know what kind of a mood she was in. If she was in a good mood, maybe they could even have a friend over, or be able to go to a movie, or spend the night at a friend's house. If she was in a bad mood, there would be chores upon chores to accomplish, all to her rigid standards, with little time for anything else.

Good moods were short but sweet, like a cooling breeze on a summer's day. Bad moods were longer and had to be weathered like storms. The first child down the stairs was the lookout to see which way the wind was blowing.

The types of abuse talked about so far have been ones of consistency. The consistent rule of the commander-in-chief. The constant yelling of the screamer. The incessant threats of the intimidator.

Roller coasters are just the opposite. They are up and down, side to side with wide mood swings. The only thing constant about them is their inconsistency.

Just like on a real roller coaster, the upswings in mood can be exhilarating and the downturns can be terrifying. Like Space Mountain at Disneyland, this is a roller coaster ride in the dark. There are no clues which way the ride is going next. You just hang on for dear life and shift whenever you can.

The up-and-down mood swings of the roller coaster rob those around him or her of any sense of peace. The house is not a haven; there are booby traps everywhere. There is no safety or security, or if there is, it happens outside the home. School is safe. Friends are safe. The roller coaster is not.

No one exists on an emotional plateau. We all have ups and downs as a part of everyday life. But a healthy self-image helps to regulate those mood swings and level out our emotional states. If we're up, we enjoy it and spread it to others. If we're down, we get through it and try not to spread it to others.

The Dr. Jekyll and Mr. Hyde

Donna lived a life of secrets. She existed in two worlds: one that encompassed her private sphere and one that encompassed her public one. On the outside she appeared competent and pleasant, not overly friendly but hardly rude in any way. People basically commented that she kept her distance. Publicly, Donna looked like she had her life together. Privately, Donna felt as if she was falling apart.

Growing up, Donna had learned to separate herself into two people. The one on the outside had it all together; the one on the inside didn't, but only came out when she was alone. The outside person was collected. The inside person was a mess.

Donna came to see me when she could no longer live two lives. Increasingly, the private person was coming out in public situations. Frustrated at not being able to maintain her composure any longer, she finally decided to try to put her halves back together.

As she shared her life with me, it became evident that Donna had learned this pattern early in life. Growing up with a strict Christian background, she'd gone to church every Sunday she wasn't sick. Her father was a leader at church, and her mother was involved in lots of church activities. Because of that, she and her siblings were expected to be always on their best behavior at church and around church people.

"Sunday best" meant more than just clothing as Donna was growing up. It meant changing how you acted. When Donna was with her father at church, he'd put his arm around her shoulders and brag about how well she was doing in school. At home, though, he would rant and rave about her failure to have A's in every subject. At church her mother spoke quietly and calmly to her, taking time in front of others to explain whatever it was she needed Donna to do. At home, her mother was short-tempered and exasperated when Donna didn't immediately understand what was expected of her.

Donna had grown up in a Dr. Jekyll and Mr. Hyde home. And just like Dr. Jekyll, she learned to conceal the identity of Mr. Hyde at all cost. No one must know she lived with a monster.

Concealment. Deception. Gentle in public—harsh in private. These are the signs of living with a Jekyll/Hyde. It could be your parents, your spouse, even yourself.

All of us fragment ourselves to some degree. We're the child, the parent, the spouse, the friend, the employer, the employee, the teacher, the lover, the loner. We can have different moods depending on where we are. We can adjust our personality to function under whatever circumstances we find ourselves. That flexibility is healthy. It's like our bodies responding to different levels of stress. Our breathing, heart rate, and blood pressure all react and change according to what is happening to us.

What is damaging is the denial of one aspect of our personality when we are functioning under another. We cannot deny we get angry whenever we're calm. We cannot deny we get sad whenever we're happy. We cannot deny we get impatient whenever we are patient. When we deny certain aspects of our personality, we experience fragmentation. Fragmentation of personality, when taken to the extreme, leads to compartmentalizing of all of life's activities. In other words, when I'm in public I can only act and feel this way, but when I'm in private I can do whatever I want. When I'm in public I'll only show a certain side of myself to others, but when I'm in private anything goes. When I'm in public I'll wear a mask of serenity, but when I'm in private I'll rip it off to show the chaos underneath. When I'm in public I'll show that I love you, but in private I'll prove it's a lie.

Living with a Jekyll and Hyde means living with mixed messages. He loves me; he loves me not; he loves me; he loves me not—except it's not flower petals he's tearing off, it's pieces of your heart. Living with a Jekyll and Hyde means living a life of secrets. No one must know what your private life is really like.

We all come as a package deal. There are going to be parts of ourselves we like and other parts we don't. A prayer by Reinhold Niebuhr goes something like this: "God, grant me the serenity to accept the things I cannot change, the courage to change the things I can, and the wisdom to know the difference." By doing this, we grant ourselves and others unconditional love. We send the message, *You don't have to be perfect for me to love you. I don't have to be perfect to love myself.*

We need to be less of a Dr. Jekyll and Mr. Hyde and more of a "what you see is what you get."

The Person Who Plays Favorites

Julie looked up and scanned the bleachers. Nope, he wasn't there yet. Taking a deep breath, she steeled herself for the fact he probably wouldn't make it . . . again. Something always seemed to come up, at least when it came to her swim meets. An unscheduled conference, a last-minute call, an unexpected rush of work.

Getting focused again on the competition, she prepared for her race. Inside, though, she was angry—angry at her father's constant failure to take time off to watch her perform. He always seemed to have time to watch her brother play football, or baseball, or whatever. He didn't always make it to every game, but enough so that he showed how important it was to him to watch Mark play.

He'd never shown up at one of her swim meets. He'd promised to "see if I can make it" a half dozen times, but every time she scanned the crowd, she never saw his face.

I'm just not as important to him as Mark is, she thought to herself, resisting that conclusion, but making it nevertheless. What else was she to think? *If I were a boy, I bet he'd watch me swim.*

Anger built up inside Julie. Anger was good; it made her swim faster. He was just never there to see it.

Few things are as devastating to a child as the realization that her parents love a sibling more than they love her. Often it isn't so much that the parents love another more, but rather they love another more easily. For whatever reason, the ability to love the other child comes more naturally.

Children are many things, but they are not stupid. They can sense when this type of inequity exists. They can sense it even when the parent does not. Desperately they attempt to figure out what is wrong with them. The reasons they come up with can cause lifelong damage to self-esteem.

There are many reasons why people will play favorites with their children. Parental expectations of what they want each child to be are applied early. Each child is judged by a certain standard. Often the first and oldest child sets that standard. Temporarily the only child, the first child is used to dealing with mostly adults from an early age and is often comfortable and deferential around adults. The other children that follow are held accountable to emulate a situation that no longer exists in the family. Expectations are not met, and comments such as, "Why can't you be more like your sister?" are the result.

It is said that opposites attract and equals repel. If you put magnets together one way, they attract quickly to each other, but turn them around and try to push them together, and they repeatedly will push off in opposite directions. Sometimes friction is caused by the very traits in the adult that are present in the child. A willful mother will butt heads with a willful daughter. A sarcastic father will clash with a mouthy son.

In healthy relationships, differences are considered strengths and are used to build up each other. Each child in a family needs to be loved and accepted for who he or she is. Healthy families encourage our unique giftedness. There is the active practicing of love, acceptance, and forgiveness.

If you grew up in an unhealthy family, you may not have come to realize what a special person you are. Finding your specialness and truly feeling it will help you to reestablish your sense of self-worth. In chapter 11 I'll share how this can happen for you.

The Role Reverser

There was no joy in Adam's voice when he talked. He answered my questions in a monotone, letting me know with every syllable how much he didn't want to be there. Adam's father, Frank, wanted him to be there. Adam's mother, Judy, really didn't care, just as long as she didn't need to pay for it. She was basically just along for the ride.

Adam lived with his mother and saw his dad every other weekend. Frank had watched his happy, laughing son slowly fade. The parents had divorced when Adam was eleven—not an easy age. He was fourteen now, and Frank was convinced something was wrong. It wasn't just a phase Adam was going through.

Talking with Judy did no good at all, Frank explained. She had just reacted violently and said he was trying to accuse her of being a bad mother. What did he know about what it was like to raise a child alone? All he had to do was take Adam a couple of days every other week. He had no idea how hard it was!

Frank had suggested having Adam start spending more time with him, but she blew up, saying the only way it would happen would be "over my dead body!"

At first Judy had been reluctant to take Adam to therapy at all, but then his grades started to suffer, and he was having trouble with kids at school. So she reluctantly agreed. Adam had no choice but to go.

For a while I just spent time with Adam, finding out what his life was like. He didn't open up right away, but that really wasn't necessary for me to see what was going on. Just a few times with him and I knew what was wrong. When Adam's parents were divorced, he'd lost his mother and his father. They had just ceased to exist.

For Judy, Adam was no longer her child. He became her companion, her confidant. She poured out on him how lonely she was feeling and how much Frank had hurt her. She told him that she wouldn't know what she would do if it weren't for him. He was all she had left in the world.

Adam cleaned the apartment whenever she was too tired, which was often. He cooked supper for them so she could unwind after work. He did the laundry, ran errands, and took care of her physical needs. Adam stopped being a child and became the parent to his mother. Their roles were all of a sudden reversed, and Adam felt the weight of adulthood before he was ready to shoulder it.

To make matters worse, Adam also lost his dad at the same time. Whenever he went to Frank's for the weekend, it was one big party. Movies, pizza, sporting events on television, and one-on-one games played outside. His dad didn't want to hear about the bad times, he just wanted his buddy back again. He wanted the Adam who played and laughed and who didn't have a care in the world. Adam stopped having a father and found a pal instead.

The pressure to provide whatever his parents needed from him was too great. Adam had to reclaim his parents and his childhood. He had to stop being his mother's caregiver and his father's buddy all of the time.

Fortunately for Adam, his parents were able to take stock and realize what they had been doing. They hadn't meant for it to happen, but it had. Together they began to rebuild their lives and reassume their proper roles.

Often the most familiar use of the role reverser is in sexual situations, where the parent, often the father, will put onto his daughter the role of lover—either physical, emotional, or both. The daughter takes on the role of the wife, providing sexual companionship. When this abuse takes an emotional form, it is often very subtle. Parent and child may appear to the outsider as having a very loving relationship. People may comment how close the two of them are.

Physical sexual relations between parent and child are called *incest*. The emotional side of such a relationship is called *emotional incest*, for the parent is using the child to fulfill his sexual needs, whether they be physical or emotional.

Role reversals can happen in other ways when the proper role within a relationship is switched. The parent becomes child. The child becomes parent. The parent becomes pal. The child becomes pal. When these roles are interfered with, needs are left unmet. A child needs to be a child, to have a parent to look to for guidance and example.

Children often enjoy reversing roles with their parents for a short time. The toddler brings Mommy her favorite blankey when she's taking a nap and tucks it lovingly under her chin like Mommy has done a hundred times for her. The adolescent pals around with his dad over the weekend, just the two of them. These reversals provide children with a glimpse of what life will be like when they're older. While children enjoy those special moments on occasion, they shouldn't have to live that way, thrust into adulthood too early and denied of childhood along the way.

The Wrath of God

"'Vengeance is mine' saith the Lord, 'I will repay!'" The preacher thumped his hand on the podium and scanned the crowd. "'All have sinned and fall short of the glory of God!' And that means all of you!" he screamed, pointing his finger randomly at the flock staring wide-eyed in front of him.

They knew the way he preached. "Fire and brimstone," they called it. They knew, and they liked it. This was the third time he'd preached for them. He'd been full of fire for the Lord each time. But lately he began to feel it was more smoke than fire. The raging passion in his gut for the Lord just wasn't there anymore. This would be the last time he preached for them, or for anyone. He just couldn't sustain the anger anymore.

Miserable, he didn't know what to do with himself. He'd let down his family, let down his church, let down his God, and let down his father. A preacher who can't preach is miserable, and so he was. A man without a pulpit, he was lost and searching for who he really was when he stepped down from the stage.

He'd always wanted to be a preacher, ever since he was a child watching his father deliver God's message to the enthralled crowd. He'd idolized his dad. His dad was on fire for the Lord in everything he did, everywhere he went. His speech was filled with Scripture references. If he did anything wrong, his dad had a verse ready to call him into the Lord's condemnation.

He was constantly reminded of how unworthy he was, of how much he had sinned, of how far he had to go to earn the love of God. He'd learned the words and the Scriptures and how to tell others about their sinful lives. He stood in the pulpit himself and sounded the warning.

It was no longer enough. He had to stop shouting long enough to listen. He had to stop feeling sorry and start feeling forgiven. He had to stop viewing his heavenly Father as an awesome representation of his earthly one—full of righteous anger with no healing grace.

He had to realize that his whole life he'd been hit over the head with the Bible. The words that had been written to bring him life instead convinced him of his death. His father had used a higher authority to rigidly enforce his own.

Slowly but surely the preacher learned about love, forgiveness, and grace. He learned to love himself and those around him. He started haltingly to show forgiveness to himself when he failed and to extend grace to others when they failed too. The wrath of God was replaced by the love of God.

For those of you who did not grow up in a religious household, this type of emotional abuse may not seem to apply. It involves the use of religion to belittle and control the behavior of others. It is most effective in use with religious cults. There is always the presentation that God is in league with your abuser. Not only are you to conform to what your abuser wants because he or she wants it, but because *God* wants it too. The score instantly becomes two to one. The deck is stacked.

Whatever wrath-of-God abusers choose to do or say is backed by their use of the higher authority. They use Scripture and religious concepts to justify their abuse. This type of emotional abuse is often combined with the commander-in-chief, who takes ultimate orders from God himself.

Faith is a beautiful thing. Connecting yourself to the power of God can be an expanding experience. It can enable you to devote yourself to a worthy goal and provide you with motivation for acts of sacrifice and service. It can give meaning to your life and provide you with purpose. Faith should never be a bludgeon. God should never be used to diminish your sense of self. Religion should not strip away your self-worth, but at its best it should contribute to your self-identity.

When actions such as hitting, throwing objects, threats, and physical intimidation are used along with verbal abuse, it reinforces the negative messages the abuse delivers. It is an abusive one-two punch. The words and the actions back each other up, creating powerful messages that need to be examined and countered. In chapter 11, we will explore how to do this. Powerful as they are, they can be replayed, both sight and sound, and put into proper perspective.

6

Emotional Abuse through Indifference

The emotional abuse talked about so far has been delivered through the sarcastic remark, the scream of rage, the whine of disappointment. We have seen it manifested in the absolute rule of law, the up-and-down flux of moods, the thoughtless actions of others. But there is another category of abuse that occurs often without a word being spoken or a finger lifted. In fact, the abuse comes about because no word is said or no action taken.

This is the emotional abuse that comes about through indifference or inaction—times when a word should be said but isn't, or an action should be taken but none is forthcoming. As damaging as the other types of emotional abuse, it is the *absence* of the expected that wounds.

With abuse through words or actions, what you expect from your abuser is substituted for something else: a kind word is replaced by a snide comment; a pat on the back is replaced by a slap across the face; a sense of belonging and security is replaced by a loss of safety and consistency.

Emotional abuse through indifference doesn't substitute any action for what might be expected from a loving, healthy relationship. Instead there is only a gaping silence, a deaf ear, a turned back. When I was growing up, this was sometimes known as "the silent treatment." It was as total a withdrawal as possible of one person from another. For whatever reason, your abuser withholds relationship from you.

A child who is ignored may engage in attention-getting activities that are destined to produce negative results. While this might seem self-defeating, the real desire is for attention. Even if the response is negative, the parent has been forced to notice the child.

None of us like to be ignored, treated as if we simply weren't important enough to notice. The person who has suffered this type of emotional abuse is saddled with the realization that his or her presence doesn't even cause a ripple in the world of the abuser. What is so damaging is that usually the abuser is someone the person desperately wants to love and notice him or her.

Children know and understand that the things adults concern themselves with are important. When parents are involved with the life of their child, they communicate to the child that he or she is important. When parents fail to become involved, they communicate to the child a sense of worthlessness.

The M.I.A. Parent

"He never wrote me, not once," Jan commented quietly, tears streaming down her face. "I kept hoping, like an idiot, every birthday, every Christmas, that I'd get something from him. I wasn't stupid enough to think he'd send a present, maybe just a card, something to show he remembered I was still alive."

Jan was thirty-six years old and struggling with her marriage. She'd already been divorced once and really wanted this second marriage to work. But Jan and her husband were having problems. They seemed to be arguing a lot. Steve, Jan's husband, said she never trusted him. She always wanted to know where he was and with whom.

"She treats me like a child," he told me in counseling. "Like she's afraid to let me out of her sight, afraid I might do something stupid."

As I talked to Jan, I realized she wasn't afraid for Steve, she was afraid for herself. Jan had been abandoned by her father at age six. Unhappy in his relationship with her mother, he'd left the state and started a new life. Jan did not figure into it. At first he'd used the excuse of the distance between them. That had worked when she was small. As the years went by with minimal contact, Jan knew he refused to see her not because he couldn't but because he really didn't want to.

Her mother had tried to console her daughter by saying it was better for both of them that he was out of their lives forever. They could go on with their lives without him around to mess things up. The thirty-six-year-old completely agreed with her mother, but the six-year-old still longed for her daddy.

Distrustful and suspicious of men, Jan had a hard time with relationships. Convinced that any man she had a relationship with might leave her at any time, she always held some of herself back so she wouldn't be hurt so badly. Overly protective and controlling, she wasn't able to relax and trust within her relationships.

"Was I so bad?" she asked out loud, to the person not even in the room with us. "Why didn't he try to see me? The only time I'll get to see my father is at his funeral. While he's alive, he doesn't want to see me. When he's dead, he won't have a choice," Jan said angrily.

"I'm not your father," Steve said softly, taking her hand. "I won't leave you like he did." Steve rocked her in his arms as the six-year-old in his wife cried.

"Why?" Jan looked up at me and asked. "What did I do that was so bad he had to go away?"

"Nothing," I told her. "It wasn't your fault he left. Jan, whatever his reasons were, it wasn't your fault."

Missing in action. No body recovered. No end to the hope that someday he might surface. No end to the pain when he never does. No closure to a wound that stubbornly refuses to heal completely.

In group sessions, when others would talk about an abusive father who would rant and rave or be so drunk he couldn't see straight, Jan would say, "At least he was there." For her it was better to be yelled at than to be forgotten. She needed to learn that neither was healthy.

Over the course of many years I have seen this type of abuse most often in fathers. They leave their families and maintain marginal contact if at all. They leave an unfinished chapter in the book of your life. The ending never gets written. No matter what other relationships are formed afterwards, the one with your father never has a resolution. There is no one to be angry with, no one to confront or accuse, and no one to whom you can say, "I forgive you, Dad."

Worst of all is the suspicion that the real reason he never came back is because you weren't special enough to him. Those who have been abandoned in this way often try to accomplish a great deal in their lives, hoping that if only they can do enough he will miraculously show up again, proud of his child at last, with some sort of plausible explanation for the years of abandonment.

Then comes that terrible moment when you have to come face-to-face with the fact that your father is a flawed, erring human being, who had troubles of his own that caused him to leave. You have to be able to accept the fact that your presence wasn't enough to override the problems of the parent who left you, whether it was substance abuse, financial irresponsibility, intense marital conflict, or just plain selfishness. Coming to grips with this difficult reality means not only do you no longer have a father, you no longer are even able to have the image of a father you so wanted and needed him to be. Sometimes reality stinks. But fantasy is no way to live your life.

As mentioned before (see the section on guilt in chapter 3, p. 34), making yourself feel responsible for your abuse is an attempt to gain control over your situation. If you can say to yourself that your parent left because of something you did, there is always the chance he might come back if you change. In order to rid yourself of this false guilt, you will need to accept the fact that he might never come back, no matter what you do. You cannot continue to make yourself responsible for his actions, to blame yourself for his leaving. Once you rid yourself of that guilt, you can begin to rebuild your sense of self-worth.

The Absent Caregiver

Jesse had pretty much gotten used to being alone all of the time. His mother never seemed to be around the apartment when he was. She usually had leftovers of some kind for him to heat up when he got home from work, but she was rarely around anymore. He was sixteen years old, and she felt he could take care of himself.

As soon as he got out of school, he'd rush over to his job as a dishwasher at a local restaurant. He'd work the rush hour, getting home around nine o'clock. Sometimes she'd be home, asleep in front of the television. At least three nights out of the week she'd be gone, partying with friends. Sometimes she'd come home late, sometimes not at all.

During the weekends there'd be errands for her to run, and he was out with his friends. They just never seemed to see each other much. Every once in a while she'd stop and say they really had to spend a night together, just the two of them, soon. But something always seemed to come up, either for her or for him.

Yes, Jesse had pretty much gotten used to being alone all of the time.

As our society changes, there seem to be more and more kids like Jesse. Housed, fed, and clothed, their physical needs are met. They have a place to sleep, even if it is often alone. They never miss a meal, even if it is leftovers eaten in an empty house. They have shoes, jeans, and baseball hats, even if there doesn't ever seem to be anyone around to notice how they look.

Unlike the M.I.A. parent, the absent caregivers aren't missing. Usually their children know exactly where they are or at least have a good idea. Absent caregivers haven't left all of the way; they just leave in spurts.

As children grow, there is the natural, normal process of establishing independence from their parents. Within healthy relationships, the parents give their children the support and guidance needed to take their first steps, knowing that those steps will eventually lead away from the parent. But the parents also keep near, for those times when their children turn around, notice how far they've gotten, and come running back to reestablish their sense of belonging and identity.

When children are small, the steps are physical ones. As children grow, more and more of those steps are emotional. It is dangerous to think that because a child is physically able to be away from the parent, he or she is well equipped to be emotionally apart as well.

With this type of abuse, parents prematurely withdraw themselves emotionally from the child. They no longer enmesh themselves in their child's emotional framework. This can be because of indifference or an overt decision to force the child to go it alone. Whatever the reason, it is abusive, for it denies children the emotional anchor from which they can explore their own identity.

It is so hard not to take our feelings of worth from other people, especially those we look to for love and relationship. It is natural to seek their acceptance and approval. If that acceptance and approval is absent, there can be two reasons: Either the acceptance and approval is being wrongly withheld, or the source of the acceptance and approval is absent altogether. In either case, gaining that acceptance and approval is difficult at best.

Is the answer then to give up trying to gain acceptance and approval completely, since it seems to be a lost cause either way? No. The answer is to open your eyes and see that there are other places to gain the acceptance and approval you need. The answer is to seek out those who won't withhold their acceptance and approval and who will maintain relationship with you and not leave. The answer is to learn to make wise choices about whom you seek your approval from and to look for support from family, friends, or the church of your choice.

The answer is to realize the one sure source of acceptance and approval who will never leave you—God.

Part Three

The
Effects
of
Emotional
Abuse

7

The Effects
on Sense
of Self

Any kind of abuse, emotional abuse included, is an attack on a person's sense of self. It demeans and controls that person through words or actions, devaluing that person and ultimately elevating the abuser. If you have suffered emotional abuse in your past or are suffering it in the present, it is not something to be ignored, denied, accepted, or perpetuated. The damage it does to your sense of self is pervasive and destructive. Over the course of my years working with the abused and those who abuse, I have found several distinct negative characteristics associated with emotional abuse:

Low self-esteem
Lack of self-confidence
Transfer of needs
Perfectionism
Inappropriate relationships
Failure syndrome

Unrealistic guilt
Crisis oriented
Unresolved anger and resentments

Depending on your situation, you may find that one or more of these effects are true in your own life. You may have been aware of these effects without understanding why they exist in your life.

Low Self-Esteem

People with high self-esteem are independent thinkers who do not merely accept someone else's word as a basis for their actions but rather evaluate the opinions of others against their own sense of who they are and what they wish to accomplish. It is not that they disregard the thoughts of others, but they do not automatically give those thoughts more value than their own.

Over time, the emotional abuser deflates your self-esteem in order to control your thoughts and actions. If you have low self-esteem, you will habitually give in to the desires and demands of others because you distrust your own ability to make competent decisions.

A person with high self-esteem is not easily controlled by someone else, especially if that someone wishes to place him or her in an oppressive position. By lowering your self-esteem, the abuser is able to link you to himself or herself by an invisible chain of fear and doubt—fear of the abuser and doubt of your ability to function apart from the abuser.

If you are suffering from low self-esteem, you may have tried unsuccessfully in the past to get beyond it. You may have even found yourself successful to some degree once you were able to remove yourself from the abusive situation. But years later, you may find yourself overreacting to an event or comment that consciously or unconsciously reminds you of the past abuse. You may have thought you were successfully over that period in your life only to have it continue to haunt you when you least expect it.

Lack of Self-Confidence

Along with low self-esteem comes a general lack of self-confidence. You may find it difficult to make decisions. After any decision is finally made, you may have second thoughts about it, even change your mind several times. Unable to make decisions on your own, you may seek out others to validate your judgment, even giving in to someone else's persuasive argument although it goes against your gut feeling.

Because of this low self-esteem and lack of self-confidence, you may purposely seek out people and work situations that do not threaten your sense of what you are able to accomplish. You may deliberately take jobs that do not stretch your abilities, choosing those you feel you can easily master and never going any further for fear of failure. Or you may find a way to avoid working with other people altogether, taking a job that infrequently brings you into contact with others. While this provides you with a sense of comfort by controlling what you are able to expect on your job, it can shortchange what you are actually able to accomplish.

Self-confidence allows people to experience risk and bounce back from the setback of failure because they have a basic belief in their own ability to learn and succeed. Low self-confidence avoids risk because of an ingrained belief that risk will always bring failure, a kind of personal Murphy's Law—"Anything I can do wrong, I will do wrong."

Transfer of Needs

All of us have a need to feel special and appreciated, to feel that we have value, to feel good about ourselves. Because of the abuse you have suffered, the fulfillment of this need to feel special and validated by those around you was absent. In order to fill that need, you learned as a child to substitute something else for it.

In my work as a counselor, I have dealt with many people who suffer from addictions of all kinds: alcohol dependency, sexual addiction, eating disorders, and drug dependency. As I have worked with these individuals to help them overcome their addictions, I often find emotional abuse as the key to their destructive patterns, especially in situations where physical or sexual abuse is absent. Too often they were the recipients of negative messages that not only robbed them of a positive sense of self but drove them to find solace in inappropriate and destructive sources.

Addictions can be as varied as the people who suffer them. Often workaholics strive to perform out of a sense of necessity, convinced they are only worth what they can accomplish, convinced they have no worth outside of the product of their labors. Instead of alcohol or drugs masking the pain they feel, they have become addicted to work (hence the name *workaholic*).

Because we are all unique individuals, our responses to filling that unmet need for approval, for validation of our personhood, will also be unique. It is important to take a look at your life and determine from what you derive your greatest sense of self-worth. If those sources have nothing to do with who you are but rather what you do, you have transferred your need to feel significant to an inappropriate area.

If you are struggling with an addiction of some kind, you may find it hard to give up because it fills a void in your life, if only for a little while. But the space you are trying to fill is probably the one that says you are special just by being you.

Perfectionism

One of the survival mechanisms a child develops to endure emotional abuse is the obsessive preoccupation with doing everything right. Since any slight or even imagined mistake on the child's part results in a negative response, the child spends a great deal of time and energy avoiding doing anything wrong that might tend to attract the attention of the abuser. The tendency toward perfectionism most often manifests itself in adulthood. This perfectionism in adults may only be directed inward, or it may be transferred outward to those around you, causing you to maintain the same expectations of perfection from others that you have for yourself.

Perfectionism can operate in two ways—both extremely destructive. You may find yourself going to any lengths to excel in whatever you do, taking up great amounts of time and energy, shortchanging your own health and peace of mind in pursuit of the perfect. You may become so focused on your performance that you completely lose sight of those around you, either coworkers or family. Driven to succeed in order to validate your own sense of self-worth, you may force all others away from you. The danger in this approach is that you are actually accomplishing a great deal, and others, removed from the adverse effects of your obsession, may praise you for how much you are able to do, reinforcing your obsessive perfectionism.

On the opposite end of this frenetic activity, your perfectionism may lead you into a state of paralysis. Since every action carries the risk of failure, actions are to be avoided. You may start projects, only to leave them lying around for weeks unfinished. As long as the project is unfinished, you haven't actually failed. You can still visualize all of the rewards of success without suffering any of the negative consequences of failure. Your life becomes a series of projects you've never started, or started but never completed.

Inappropriate Relationships

Because your early relationships were dysfunctional, your ability to maintain positive relationships in adulthood may

be compromised. You may attempt to reinvent your old dysfunctional relationships in your new ones, choosing individuals who will again place you in the role of the abused.
On the other hand, your dysfunctional responses within a
relationship may make any relationship more difficult to
maintain.

The emotional abuser succeeds when he or she is able to
replace your own control over yourself with the abuser's control. You no longer trust yourself but instead allow the abuser
to hold undue influence over your thoughts and actions. The
abuser becomes, in essence, a part of you, controlling you
and how you view yourself and your world. The boundary
where you start and the abuser ends is blurred.

In subsequent relationships you may find yourself completely giving in to the other person, totally submerging yourself in the other person's personality, accepting his or her view
of the world and of you. Unfortunately, you may seek someone who is dominant and controlling with whom to establish a relationship. The roles in this new relationship will fit
into a predictable pattern.

On the other hand, you may be extremely sensitive to anything you think seems remotely like control—even commitment. It may be difficult for you to maintain intimate relationships because the giving necessary to have intimacy may
trigger a highly negative response on your part. You may only
feel comfortable in a relationship where there is a deliberate
lack of commitment, having decided that no one will ever
have that much control over you again.

Additionally, you may be very suspicious of anyone who
seeks to get to know you in a deep, personal way. You may
erect elaborate barriers to keep people out or construct tests
of those who seek a relationship with you to determine their
real motives.

Finally, there is a danger of becoming extremely self-
absorbed. If your experience has always been that whatever
you did or didn't do brought an immediate, extreme reac-

tion, you may have concluded that the world really did, in effect, revolve around you. You may have developed the habit of analyzing everything that happens around you as it relates to you, whether it really does or not.

While these tactics helped you survive your abuse, they have left you ill-prepared to operate within healthy, positive relationships. Attempting to submerge yourself completely into a healthy relationship may make you appear possessive and clingy, suffocating the other person in your need to meld your individuality with his or hers. On the other hand, a suspicion of intimacy and a general aloofness may dissuade most others from even attempting a relationship with you. And being extremely self-absorbed leaves little room for thoughts of others. (See chapter 9 for a further discussion of emotional abuse and its effect on your pattern of relationships.)

Failure Syndrome

During the 1984 presidential election, a little-known politician from Colorado soon emerged as the shining hope for the Democratic party. He was ruggedly good-looking, spoke with sincerity and intelligence, and seemed to articulate the environmental awareness many felt was needed in American politics. His name was Gary Hart.

But a funny thing happened on the way to the election. Stories began to surface about his marital infidelities. Slowly they began to erode some of his support as people questioned his moral character. His wife staunchly stood by his side and denied the stories. Hart even challenged reporters to catch him in the act—and they did. Reporters photographed a young woman entering and leaving Hart's townhouse late at night.

Hart's ratings began to plummet as people shook their heads in wonder. Why would Gary Hart flaunt his indiscretions in front of the public and press? And especially at so critical a time as a national election? One explanation surfaced that was intriguingly different from the rest: Gary Hart was suffering from a failure syndrome. This syndrome meant that deep down Gary Hart didn't feel he was good enough to win, so he subconsciously sabotaged his own campaign by engaging in conduct he knew would cost him the election. The article that appeared in the paper touting this explanation cited other examples in Hart's life, all the way back to high school, when he had done something so obviously wrong it seemed as if he wanted to throw away whatever chances he had at succeeding in a given task.

In my work I have found that many people we would consider successful feel deep down as if they have cheated somehow to get where they are. Feeling they don't deserve their success, they live with a constant fear that any day they are going to be exposed for what they really are—frauds, totally inadequate for their jobs. They fear their success was simply a fluke and that eventually the truth will catch up to them and they will ultimately fail in humiliation.

The tragedy is these are truly capable, often highly creative people who distrust their own success. And the reason they distrust their success is because someone convinced them during their life, most likely in childhood, that they weren't worth anything and were destined for failure.

Even though you've worked hard to get where you're at today, do you still worry that it will all be taken away from you? Do you worry deep down inside that you'll be asked to handle a job that is so far beyond your abilities everyone will finally see how you've been fooling them all these years? Has the stress of waiting for the other shoe to drop become so intense that you have, like Gary Hart, simply taken off one of your own shoes and dropped it yourself? Has the act of failure become easier to bear than the constant strain of impending doom?

If you find yourself doing or saying things that you know will jeopardize your job situation or your relationships and then find yourself at a loss to explain why you would act in such a way, you may be operating under a failure syndrome.

Unrealistic Guilt

This is the effect of emotional abuse that constantly causes you to say, "It's all my fault," and you do mean *all*. So ingrained is the belief that you are to blame for the world's problems that you carry around an oppressive load of guilt about real and imagined shortcomings.

The negative messages relayed to you from your abuser squarely put you to blame for whatever problem he or she seemed to be having. If she had trouble sleeping, it was because you were keeping her awake. If he failed at a sales presentation, it was because your lousy mood destroyed his concentration. If she couldn't find whatever she was looking for, it was because you hid it.

You heard over and over again how your actions soured the life of your abuser, so you came to feel guilty for every bad thing that happened to those around you. If your son had a flat tire on his way to work, it happened because you didn't check the tread life on his tires. If your daughter broke up with her boyfriend, it was because you didn't give her just the right advice she needed. If your spouse got a traffic ticket, it was because you sent him or her out to the store to run a quick errand.

With this guilt comes the fear that you'll keep doing things to hurt those you really love. You constantly apologize for wrongs and don't really believe it when the response is, "Don't worry. It's not your fault." Deep down you are convinced that it *is* your fault. Things would have turned out so differently if only you had done something else.

Crisis Oriented

Often emotional abuse takes the form of placing the abused in the position of having to save the abuser. After all, your abuser has made you feel that whatever is wrong is your fault. If it's your fault, it must be your responsibility to fix it. You then desperately try to win back your abuser's favor by fixing whatever problem the abuser seems to be having. The child who is emotionally neglected by his mother may find the only way to be with her is when he's acting as her buddy or confidant. The person whose father is an abusive alcoholic may only hear words of thanks or apology when she's carrying him to his bed or cleaning up his vomit.

As an adult, the abused person becomes crisis oriented, thriving on being the one who fixes everything. If crises don't happen regularly enough to satisfy the need to rush in and act as the knight in shining armor, the abused person may create crises, or blow up normal, everyday events or problems into crises of immense proportions.

If you are crisis oriented, you may find it provides you with a sense of significance. For a while it may even bring you accolades, positive attention, and gratitude. But people can only handle so many crises before they get tired of them, and of you manufacturing them. They may become so hardened to your manufactured crises that they fail to appreciate any real ones.

Crisis oriented people feel in control when they are managing a crisis. Because of their dysfunctional past, they may have had a life of crises growing up. They have learned improperly that crises are normal, crises are manageable, crises are energizing, and therefore crises are necessary.

Unresolved Anger and Resentments

Underlying so many effects of emotional abuse is unresolved anger that stems from:

the seething, violent sense that you've been treated unfairly

the sure knowledge that no matter how hard you tried, it never made any difference

the terrible fear that it was really all your fault they treated
you that way
the debilitating realization you were an idiot to think and
hope that someday they'd change

Because the emotional abuse has been overlooked and
ignored for so long, it has been difficult to give a reason for
all of your anger. This anger has been left unresolved because
its source has gone unrecognized.

Unresolved anger has a way of venting, even if it spews in
inappropriate directions. One of the telltale signs of emotional abuse I look for is if the person has a tendency to suddenly erupt in anger at inconsequential events. There is an
adage, "An *odd* reaction is an *old* reaction." And the saying,
"The straw that broke the camel's back," presupposes there
was an awful lot of straw loaded on that camel's back before
the last piece finally broke it.

If you have been emotionally abused in the past, you could
be carrying around a load of straw you aren't even aware of.
The tendency to erupt in anger is a signpost of a deeply sensitive, hurting place in your life—an emotional bruise that
causes you to wince every time it is touched.

All of these effects of emotional abuse have come about
through the verbal and nonverbal messages you have received
from those who were abusing you. These messages caused
you to doubt yourself. They have sabotaged your sense of
self. They made you afraid of your own shadow, cautious and
suspicious of the people around you. They have subtly influenced your ability to have a positive relationship with yourself. They also have affected your ability to establish and maintain positive relationships with others.

8

The
Physical Effects

Catherine was having an affair. It was her little secret. No one else was let in on it, not even her best friend. Her husband didn't know, of course. Every time she'd meet with her lover, she knew it was wrong. Her lover met needs she had in the way nothing else seemed to. Even though she'd feel dirty afterwards, it didn't stop her from going. They'd meet in quiet rooms in out-of-the-way places where no one knew her. She devised elaborate lies to cover up what she was doing.

It wasn't just the time she spent with her lover. Even when they were apart, her mind was on her beloved: when they would meet, what they would do together, how it would feel when it was just the two of them alone again. As she thought of their time together, she could almost begin to hate what they did enough to stop. But life without her lover seemed like no life at all.

It might have been different if Catherine's lover had been a man, but Catherine was a bulimic, and her lover was food—

preferably sweets, chocolate in particular. She'd find a safe place, away from prying eyes, and consume mass quantities of cakes, cookies, donuts, desserts of any kind. Shoving them down her throat as fast as she could, she felt as if her hunger was just on the verge of being satisfied. It was always on the verge, though. So she'd stuff more and more down in the hope of achieving fulfillment.

Afterwards, she'd panic. Finding a bathroom, she'd turn on the water full blast to hide the noise and stick her finger down her throat.

Something inside Catherine's mind drove her to act out this destructive scenario over and over with her body. Not content to keep the abusive effects to itself, the mind was determined to take the body along with it.

Earlier I talked about how fear, guilt, and anger combine in emotional abuse to damage a person (see chapter 3). Up until now, the damage described has been primarily emotional or mental. But it is important to remember that our minds and bodies are linked. What we feel emotionally, we experience physically.

All of us have felt heart-pounding horror at some event, like walking down a dark, deserted street and suddenly hearing footsteps behind you. Your heart races, your respiration quickens, your muscles tense. Adrenaline flows into your system, supercharging you for action. You experience the fight-or-flight response to stimulus.

When this response becomes less an occasional occurrence and more a way of life, there are bound to be physical effects on the body. In my work with a variety of disorders, I have found that each of these different emotions—fear, anger, and guilt—are felt in specific areas of the body, as if each emotion takes up residence in a particular room.

Fear is most often experienced in the stomach. This can be referred to as a gut reaction. Anger appears to be located in the head. The face turns red, blood vessels become distended and pop out, sweat pores enlarge, and breathing increases. Guilt seems to produce an overall bodily reaction.

Through my work I've been able to identify certain physical conditions that indicate to me the presence of emotional abuse as well as other types of abuse:

Addictions
Allergies/asthma
Depression
Digestive disturbances
Eating disorders
Free-floating anxiety
Hypochondria
Migraine headaches
Panic attacks
Phobias
Unexplained skin rashes

Emotional abuse produces stress in the individual. Fear, guilt, and anger produce anxiety, frustration, and hopelessness. When these emotions and feelings are constantly present, the body reacts by producing chemicals designed to stimulate the body to either fight or flight. Because often neither of these responses is appropriate to the situation, the body has to deal with the chemical aftermath these emotions can produce.

Addictions

Emotional abuse leaves deep hurting places in the inner-being of the abused. Your abuse may have left you feeling fearful, guilty, and angry over what happened to you. These are unpleasant emotions at best, and destructive, harmful emotions at worst. One way many have found to combat the harmful effects of these emotions is to cover over them with a physical addiction to any of a variety of substances.

Alcoholism and drug use can provide what seems to be a

way of numbing the pain you feel. Pain fades and memory fades when under the influence of the drug of your choice. The relief from pain produces pleasure, but there's always a morning after for the night before. Whatever numbing or pleasurable feeling achieved is only temporary. So the behavior must be repeated, over and over, to provide even temporary relief. With many addictive substances, the body begins to tolerate the drug, forcing a higher dosage to be used each time to achieve the same effect, thus feeding the addiction further.

In addition to alcohol and drugs, people can also become addicted to food, to sex, to work—anything that allows them to travel outside of themselves for a while, to forget who they really are and how they feel.

The compounding problem of so many physical addictions is they begin as a direct response of the mind to combat an emotional trauma and end up involving the body as well. Now, not only do you have the emotional abuse to work through, you also have the physical addiction to recover from as well.

Allergies/Asthma

Recent evidence has shown that many allergies, especially to molds, can be triggered by stress. Allergies are an inappropriate reaction of the body's immune system to foreign matter. In other words, the body incorrectly identifies mold, dust, pollen, or a food substance as a threat to the body and triggers the arsenal of its immune system to combat the enemy. All the body's defenses rush to force the intruder out of the body. The eyes swell with tears, flushing out impurities. The nose begins to run and you sneeze, blowing the nasal passages clear. The throat becomes ticklish and you cough, forcing the lungs clear. The heart begins to beat faster, increasing circulation.

A positive correlation exists between feelings of stress and allergic reactions. It is as if the body is on alert, so sensitive to any change in condition that it begins to attack substances that normally would be considered benign.

Likewise, asthma has been linked to high levels of stress in individuals, especially those dealing with perfectionism. The anger and feelings of resentment present in those who suffer from perfectionism constantly force the body into a state of alert, often triggering an asthmatic attack.

A woman I dealt with came to me on the recommendation of a medical doctor. She was experiencing trouble breathing. It got to the point where she was gasping for breath at the slightest exertion. She felt something was medically wrong, but the doctor had been unable to find an organic cause for the tightness in her chest. He felt there had to be a psychological explanation for her physical problem, so he sent her to me.

As I talked with her, I found out she lived in a very abusive relationship with a husband who beat her and her children. Not only did he beat her physically, he also beat her up emotionally. She could do nothing right, say nothing right. Her life from morning to night was filled with fear and anxiety. Subconsciously she focused the stress she was feeling into her throat and lungs.

The doctor who sent her to me said, "I can't find anything to explain this closing of her air passages, but if something doesn't change, she'll suffer respiratory failure within a year."

She was trying so hard to keep all of her feelings bottled up inside that she was slowly suffocating herself. Over the course of that year, I was able to help her realize what her mind was doing to her body. Then she was able to express the anger and frustration she was feeling instead of bottling it up inside.

Depression

Depression has been described as a deep, black hole you find yourself falling into. The sides are steep and slick. There doesn't seem to be any way to stop your descent. It happens in slow motion. The flailing of the arms, the twists and turns of the body—agonizing movements that produce no results. Eventually, you stop fighting and just slide down into the pit. No light. No desires. No energy. No hope. But also no pain. No anger. No emotions to deal with at all. Just a numbing grayness hanging over your life. When pain is too great, when anger too consuming, when emotions too conflicting, the blurry haze of depression has an allure.

Emotional abuse leads to intense feelings of anger, rage, resentment, and bitterness. Submerged feelings of guilt and fear of your abuser can lead you to choose a safer target for your anger than your abuser. All too often, that target is yourself. Unspent anger continually works inside the body, using up energy, causing feelings of fatigue and apathy. Unable to see any hope in your life, you slowly begin to isolate yourself from others, from getting out and socializing, from exercising or taking care of your body. So often in your abuse nothing has seemed to work. Every time you thought it was going to get better, it got worse. So what's the use, you wonder.

This world we live in can be a difficult place. There are pressures and stresses that come from everyday living that are enough to temporarily sideline even the healthiest of us. When emotional abuse has battered your defenses, maintaining a successful stand against those forces can be almost impossible. That is why it is so important to gain support and strength from others: from healthy relationships, from friends who love you, even from caring professionals who can assist you in rediscovering your strength to face each day successfully. You may also need a professional to assist you in rebalancing your body's natural chemistry when necessary.

Digestive Disturbances

Our digestive systems are made up of an enormous network of muscles and chemicals, all working in harmony to process the foods we eat. When you find yourself under stress, muscles all over the body begin to contract and knot. Chemical levels in the bloodstream are altered. Is it any wonder, then, that so many people experience stress in their stomachs? Heartburn, acid indigestion, gas, and ulcers can all be physical signs of emotional stress.

Of course, these symptoms can have very real physical causes, but in our hectic, fast-paced lives, we too often don't eat what we should. We also don't take time to relax when we eat. This stress on our bodies can produce digestive problems. Compounding that are the food allergies we can develop because of our eating patterns. Too much fat, sugar, and wheat products, which are so plentiful in modern processed food, can trigger an overload in our systems, producing an allergic reaction to those and other substances.

A person who has been emotionally abused isn't used to being completely relaxed. The abused must always be on the lookout for the abuser. Fear of the abuser haunts every moment. Muscles rarely relax; underlying or overt muscular tension is always present. Digestive juices continue to churn, even if there is no food to digest. Eventually this leads the stomach to, in essence, digest itself. When it does so, holes in the stomach lining result, producing ulcers.

Eating Disorders

Bulimia, anorexia, and compulsive overeating all have their roots in abuse of some kind. They derive from an inappropriate use of control. The bulimic and the compulsive overeater are out of control. The compulsive overeater is a binger, like the bulimic, without the subsequent purging. For the anorexic, the problem isn't a lack of control, it is the obsessive use of control—specifically control over one's consumption of food.

No one starts out life deciding they are going to spend years of their life stuffing sweets and junk food down their throats only to throw it back up or flush it out of the body with laxatives and diuretics. No one starts out life deciding they are only going to drink water and take four bites of food all day, forcing their body to shrink down farther and farther. No one starts out that way.

I have rarely found elsewhere the intensity of anger that I find in anorexics. After a period of slow starvation, it seems as if the anger is the only thing fueling their shrunken bodies. Their eyes burn with it. Jaws remain clenched with it. The rigid control they exert over their own ability to feel hunger is their compulsive attempt to control their anger. Control their hunger—control their bodies—control their anger.

Somewhere along the line, messages were given to all these individuals about their self-worth, their looks, their weight, their value to themselves and others. Those messages, delivered under the battering of emotional abuse, gave birth to the destructive practices of the eating disorder.

Free-Floating Anxiety

I have people come to me complaining of a general sense of unease, of impending doom, but without a real cause behind it. They most often are highly pessimistic in nature and bitter about what life has dealt them. Sure of disaster around the next corner, they generally have a way of finding it. Unsure about their ability to make decisions, they feel as if something bad is about to happen to them.

Living with emotional abuse sets up a pattern where nothing is safe, no moment is left unguarded. Everyone must be watched. All precautions must be taken. Every contingency must be planned for. This makes for an individual who is always on guard.

Often they are called high-strung or nervous types. What they are experiencing is a continual state of anxiety. If the abused is no longer in an abusive situation, the reason for the anxiety no longer exists, but the pattern remains. Without a focus, it remains free-floating—a constant sense of apprehension without a concrete source.

The fear of the abuse has become a permanent feature, etched on the inner-being of the abused. If fear was the one strong emotion you grew up with, if fear proved useful to you in the past by alerting you to danger, then fear becomes a normal way of processing information in the present.

Hypochondria

For some people, this free-floating anxiety can eventually lodge in their bodies, causing a variety of physical discomforts. Often they experience chronic symptoms that elude medical diagnosis. It is obvious to them they have a problem, but their doctor is unable to find it. Too often in the past, mood-altering drugs have been prescribed to calm such a case of nervousness.

With hypochondria there are a multitude of physical complaints, usually minor and not life threatening, that plague a person. Sometimes hypochondria can manifest itself in a disease-of-the-month syndrome. You read of someone who experienced a particular disease, a certain symptom, and sure enough, you find you have it too.

Such preoccupation with your own body and physical health leads to a hyperfocus on every ache and pain, pimple, and twinge you may have. It provides an outlet for the free-floating fear and anxiety.

Migraine Headaches

Blood is pounding in your head. Your temples feel like they're about to explode. Any amount of light sends piercing stabs of pain through your eyes. Movement is nauseating, sound unbearable. The only way to cope is to lie perfectly still. No light. No sound. No movement. Only a slow countdown until the pain diminishes enough for you to realize you're going to live, or even want to.

One of the most debilitating responses of the body to stress is a migraine headache. Silent stalkers, they attack unannounced, rendering you incapable of tolerating stimulus of any kind. There's no way to work around this effect. It knocks you flat on your back and keeps you there.

Researchers are still studying why stress triggers this reaction. But it has been associated with low self-esteem, extreme perfectionism, and the accompanying feelings of anger, fear, and guilt. Much more work needs to be done to understand and treat these intense and painful episodes.

Low self-esteem and perfectionism are two characteristics of people who have undergone prolonged emotional abuse in their past. In my work I've found that migraine headaches are, unfortunately, another.

Panic Attacks

It all started with an elevator. Janice was taking the elevator up to her usual floor at work one day when the elevator malfunctioned. She was trapped inside for hours until someone was finally able to get it working properly again.

As hard as that was to overcome, Janice was beginning to put it behind her and get a proper perspective on the traumatic event when lightning struck a second time. Janice loved to go to the Space Needle restaurant in downtown Seattle. It was a favorite place of hers to take out-of-town friends. Towering high over the city, the restaurant afforded a revolving view of the skyline as you dined.

In order to get to the restaurant circling atop the Space Needle, you have to go up in an elevator that has windows along its side so you can enjoy the view on your way up. On Janice's way up, the elevator broke. Twice in as many months Janice had to endure the trauma of being trapped in a nonfunctioning elevator. This time the elevator had windows, so she could see just how dangerous a position she was in.

For a while afterwards she was able to go on with her life. But soon she found the thought of even stepping into an elevator was nauseating. Instead she took the stairs. But then even the thought of being up that high, no matter how she got there, caused intense attacks of panic. Her heart would race. She would become dizzy and light-headed, and she would hyperventilate. Eventually she was forced to give up her job, physically no longer able to make it to the twelfth floor.

When Janice finally came to see me, she couldn't even travel up a flight of stairs without having a panic attack. The attacks were so strong she was sure she was going to die of a heart attack. She had a two-story house, but she started sleeping on the sofa downstairs to avoid climbing above ground level.

Janice had always been a high-strung person. When she was a child, her father was commanding and her mother was demanding. She'd grown up very performance driven. Everything needed to be done just so with Janice. Her looks, her dress, her manners, and her work were carried out with precision and control. Until she lost control twice in the elevators.

Panic attacks can come anytime, though usually they seem to hit young adults. All of a sudden a traumatic event happens, and it sets up a pattern. The place or circumstance of the attack is to be scrupulously avoided. Any hint that a panic attack might come makes one a certainty. The free-floating anxiety of emotional abuse seems to take hold not in the body, as in the case of hypochondria, but in a traumatic event. The fear of it happening again merely adds to the anxiety and increases the likelihood of its reoccurrence.

With proper insight into her personality and by treating her whole person, Janice was able to confront her fear of heights and slowly, inch by inch, regain a foothold in the world.

Phobias

Anxiety can manifest itself in different ways, tied to different events, running the gamut from acrophobia (fear of heights) to claustrophobia (fear of enclosed spaces) to agoraphobia (fear of open spaces). Often these phobias are as unique as the individual. Some others are arachnophobia (fear of spiders) and pyrophobia (fear of fire).

Most of the time these disorders can be treated by going back and discovering the root event that triggered the panic response and then putting it back into perspective. Then slowly, with support, you can overcome your fears a step at a time.

Unexplained Skin Rashes

Have you or anyone you know broken out in hives before an important event? Or did your skin break out in pimples or acne the day before the senior prom? Or have you developed a rash all over your face before a sales presentation?

The skin is a canvas on which our inner emotional state is often painted. Healthy, glowing skin can be a sign of a contented, at-peace individual. Erupting, pimply skin may be a sign of inner turmoil, as any teenager would attest.

This is not always the case, though, and there are certainly physical reasons for the skin to break out without emotional issues playing a part. In my work, however, I have found that as individuals are undergoing counseling, they may develop skin problems at particularly stressful times in their recovery.

The effects of emotional abuse rarely remain in the realm of the mental or emotional alone. Invariably, they spread to the other aspects of a person as well. The physical body is tied to your emotional state. If you are a happy, contented person, your body tends to thrive. If you are an anxious, driven person, your physical body suffers. While you might choose to ignore the signs of emotional abuse in your life, often you have no choice but to pay attention to the physical ones. When the body speaks, it's time to listen. Even if it speaks in a whisper, don't wait until it begins to shout. You may want to consider medical and psychological assistance. By being alert to one part of your self, your body, and the effects you experience, you can be led to discover the truth about your whole self—emotional, physical, and relational.

9

The Effects on Relationships

Emotional abuse starts within the framework of a re-lationship with a parent, a sibling, a friend, a teacher, or an employer. The relationships we form with others are meant to give us support, establish a sense of belonging and unity, and fill our emotional and physical needs for comfort and companionship. When abuse is present in our relationships, these needs are not being met and physical or emotional damage is being done.

If you have been involved in an abusive relationship, you may have an inaccurate perception of what makes a good relationship. And because we often tend to go toward the familiar, it should not be surprising that an abusive past relationship can set you up for an abusive present or future relationship.

When emotional abuse damages one relationship, it can affect all of the relationships you form. Most importantly, it can damage the relationship you have with yourself. It can also be especially damaging to your family relationships, and it can damage the relationships you have with friends or coworkers. Emotional abuse can also have a detrimental effect on your spiritual relationship with God.

The Relationship with Self

The world is quiet. No sound from the television to mask inner thoughts. No music from the radio to drown out the cries of the past. No light to distract the inner eye from seeing the way things really are. No presence of other people to overshadow the knowledge of self. Just the late-night/early-morning moment of truth when the only person left to hide from is looking back at you from the mirror.

In chapter 7 I discussed in depth the negative effects emotional abuse can have on your sense of self. How you feel about yourself is the backbone of your relationship with self. If you feel good about who you are as an individual, your relationship with self is supportive and based on realistic expectations. If you have believed the false messages fed to you through abusive people, your relationship with self is fraught with self-doubt, guilt, and frustration.

You can never run away from yourself. You can try, but you will always catch up with yourself in those quiet moments just before dawn when the world is silent and there's no place left to hide. Every time you look in a mirror you're forced to see who you are. And just as there are mirrors for your eyes, there are mirrors for your soul—those times and events when you truly see who you are.

One of the most damaging things about emotional abuse is that it distorts your vision. It causes you to see a false reflection in the mirror. It causes you to distrust what your eyes see and your heart feels deep down. In the darkest moments, when you have isolated yourself from everyone else around you, how you feel about yourself still remains. The relationship with self affects all other relationships you have.

Your Relationship with Your Spouse

Too often the sad truth is that the emotional abuse you have been subjected to was from a member of your own family. Gone was the ideal "Ozzie and Harriet" family with a loving set of parents and close-knit siblings. Instead something else—something far less ideal—was substituted.

You may have thought that when you grew up, you were over it, that you had escaped from your situation and left it behind you. Often this is not the case. There are very specific ways that emotional abuse in the past can affect present or future relationships within your adult family.

One of the manifestations of your abuse may be your desire to find a person just like the one who abused you. While this may not seem to make much sense logically, it certainly holds true emotionally. Relationships can be scary. The other person and how he or she will feel and react is an unknown quantity. Often, to cut down on the amount of surprise, people look for personality traits with which they are most familiar. If the person who emotionally abused you was a parent of the opposite sex, the chances are you may be drawn to a mate who portrays similar characteristics. If you had a controlling father, you may seek out a man who is opinionated and overbearing. If you had a loud, outspoken mother, you may look for a woman who exhibits the same characteristics. While it is said that opposites attract, there are complex reasons why one person falls in love with another. Subconsciously you may have chosen a mate who mirrors behavior within your new relationship that you are familiar with from a past one.

Unfortunately, this could mean entering into another abusive relationship, with an abusive spouse taking the place of an abusive parent. The emotional abuse in your past may cause you to make inappropriate choices in relationships in the present or future. This is one part of the repeating cycle of abuse, going from one abusive relationship to another.

On the other hand, you may have been able to avoid this pattern by intentionally choosing someone who was nothing like your past abuser. Making this choice, you may have thought you were off the hook. This is not necessarily the case. Even if your current mate is free from abusive behavior, your abusive past can adversely affect your relationship.

Jack watched his wife move around the room. She was gorgeous—beautifully dressed, slim, and tan. He watched the other men watching her. A few gave her lecherous glances, but most were frankly appreciative of what they saw. Part of him felt a sense of pride that he had such a beautiful wife. He knew there were many in the room who wondered, ever so briefly, what it would be like to be in his shoes.

If they only knew, he thought to himself. It wasn't that he didn't love Pat. He did. And it wasn't that he didn't appreciate her physical beauty, because he did. But none of the others in the room knew what it was like to live with her.

Pat never dropped her guard. Always in control of every situation, she lived her life firmly in command. Her daily schedule was totally regimented. She knew what she was doing nearly every second of every day.

Her appearance was also strictly regulated. Hours were spent maintaining her sleek, healthy look. She was always immaculate in appearance. Every aspect of her wardrobe was chosen with the greatest care, and at no small cost, he had to add. She would fly into a rage about a hair out of place or a pound gained overnight. If she was happy with her appearance, she could smile. If she wasn't, the most she could muster was a polite, bland expression in public and a tight, closed demeanor in private.

Her food intake was maintained with near obsessive diligence. He might indulge in a late-night snack or occasional hot fudge sundae, but she never did. Meals weren't a relaxing time to mull over the day together. To Pat they were brief skirmishes to be won as quickly as possible. He usually ended up finishing his meal alone, while Pat flew around the kitchen removing all traces of the dinner.

He couldn't burp, pass gas, pick his teeth, or, God forbid, pick his nose anywhere near Pat. She felt natural bodily functions were crude. There wasn't anything relaxing about being around Pat. She was always in control, always accomplishing something, and she expected him to live his life the same way. There was no end to the disappointment he caused Pat when he didn't. He heard about it constantly.

Their sex life was totally controlled by Pat and whether she was in the mood. Since he would never even think of encouraging her when she wasn't in the mood, she always decided when they would have sex. It was a given that he wanted to—a point she made sure to bring up derisively whenever provoked. So whenever she wanted to have sex, he was expected to comply, which, quite honestly, wasn't enough for him. But he loved Pat and waited patiently for those times when she wanted to love him back.

Others saw the Pat she so meticulously presented. He lived with the parts that were left. So he sat back and watched her move around the room, engaging in as much wishful thinking as any man there.

One of the most common relational effects of emotional abuse I have found is an inability to experience intimacy. At the heart of the ability to maintain intimacy is trust. An intimate relationship is one that leaves little room to hide. You open yourself up as completely as you can to another person. The more open you are, the more you can join together.

Abuse destroys trust. In the past, trusting an abusive person only led to pain. Trust, therefore, is something to be avoided, to be suspicious of. But trust is an integral component to a healthy marriage. When it is absent, the relationship suffers.

Within a sexual relationship, the need for trust is crucial. When problems are present in the sexual life of a couple, they tend to multiply into other areas as well. The frustrations of being sexually fearful or unfulfilled can spill over into hurt feelings and repressed anger.

Another damaging offshoot of emotional abuse is perfectionism. Wanting to do things well is hardly a character flaw, but perfectionism is the obsessive need to operate at a perfect level at all times. If this level is not achieved, the perfectionist can react with either extreme anger or apathetic indifference. Either, "I don't care what you do, I'm not leaving until I get this right," or "What difference does it make anyway, I'll never get it right, so why bother trying at all?"

Perfectionists put themselves under tremendous pressure at all times. Things must be done to their rigid standards or their whole world comes crashing down. Anyone who happens to be near them often gets caught in the crash.

Terry was furious. Her new husband, Brent, was nothing but negative about her new job. When she came home excited about the promotion, he'd brought up every reason he could think of why the job really wasn't all that great. She'd expected him to be excited! After all, it meant a considerable increase in her salary. More money for her meant more money for him, so what was the problem anyway? In a fit of anger, she'd even accused him of being jealous. Nothing else seemed to make sense.

She'd fumed out of the apartment, intent on a nice long drive to blow off some steam. How dare he put her down like that! What was his problem anyway? She'd expected a happy, supportive reaction from him and had gotten the exact opposite. Why did he react in such a negative way? Had she really misjudged him so completely? And what did that mean for the future, *their* future?

Brent couldn't believe it when she'd slammed out the door. Why in the world had he said what he did? Terry had worked hard for that promotion. She deserved it. It meant more financial freedom for the two of them. Why did he have such an uneasy feeling wash over him when she'd delivered the news? It was like he was afraid of something, but he couldn't figure out what. All he knew was Terry telling him about the job had made him feel scared . . . more than scared—unsafe.

Alone in the quiet apartment, Brent began to backtrack in his mind to the root of his uneasy feeling. He closed his eyes and tried to remember when he'd felt that way before. At first, nothing came—no sights, no sounds, no memories at all. He felt himself becoming tense again. Letting out a deep breath, he told himself that it was okay. He moved his neck back and forth trying to relax. Still nothing came.

He tried another tactic. Holding a conversation with himself, he asked himself, "What's the worst thing that could happen if Terry takes this job?" As soon as he asked it, he had his answer. "She'll leave you," popped into his head so quickly and so clearly he nearly jumped out of his chair.

"You think she won't need you anymore!" he said to himself in amazement.

By the time Terry returned home, her anger spent but her confusion remaining, Brent was able to sit her down and explain where his fear had come from. Brent's parents had divorced when he was twelve. He didn't see much of his dad after that. They had seen each other a few times and talked on the phone, but his dad had seemed to get along just fine without him, his mom, and sister. When Brent's dad left, Brent wasn't entirely sad to see him go. Brent's dad had always had a sharp tongue. In the twelve years before he left the family, Brent could probably count on one hand the number of times his dad had said anything nice to him. Brent never seemed to be able to live up to his father's expectations. Consequently, his father was convinced Brent wouldn't ever amount to much.

About the only thing Brent's dad thought he did right was to marry Terry. He came to the wedding after not seeing or speaking to Brent in years. But he had come, and Brent distinctly remembered him saying, "Never thought you'd ever find anyone as good as Terry. You just make sure you keep her."

Deep down Brent was afraid he wouldn't be able to.

Terry cried when he told her what was really going on inside him. She hugged him close and promised never to leave him, ever. The job was important to her, sure, but he was the most important thing in her life and always would be.

"Stop listening to your dad," she said sternly, while holding him close, "and start listening to me!"

Even if you've married a so-called healthy person and avoided the trap of continuing in an abusive relationship, it doesn't necessarily mean that your own past will have no repercussions in your new relationship. Brent and Terry were a couple who came to me for counseling. Brent needed guidance to overcome his feelings of abandonment and low self-esteem. Terry needed help to understand Brent and how his abusive past was affecting their present relationship. Terry was not a victim of emotional abuse in her life, but when she married Brent she became joined emotionally and physically with someone who was.

As I have said, emotional abuse triggers intense feelings of fear, guilt, and anger. Those emotions can be denied and repressed for years. But eventually they have a way of expressing themselves, often in inappropriate and confusing ways to both the abused person and those in relationship with him or her.

One of the most common responses is that of hypersensitivity. Because of an abusive past, you may have developed a radar system tuned to picking up any comment or action from those around you that could be interpreted as being negative. If you grew up in a negative environment, that is what you have come to expect and anticipate. You look for the negative and can usually find it.

When you then react to the negative things you perceive in the actions and comments of others, it is often with an increased response. Your anger is all consuming. You aren't just angry about what was said yesterday, but you're angry at all the hurtful things that were said in all the past yesterdays.

Your guilt is overwhelming. What they said about you the other day was so true. It's been true all your life. Why even try to deny it anymore? You're bad. You're nothing. Why even try anymore?

The emotional responses you feel are very real, even though they may be based in a large part on past events. Those you are in a relationship with may have no frame of reference for your strong reactions. They simply won't understand why what they said or did caused you to react the way you did, often you won't either. It can add tension and confusion to your relationships.

Relationships on the Job

In chapter 7 I have already discussed the failure syndrome as it applies to work situations. It can leave you fearful of being discovered as a fraud or cause you to take jobs that are not challenging to you.

In addition, your working relationships can be affected if the personalities of your boss or coworkers closely approximate someone in your past who emotionally abused you. Your boss could be just like your dad. A supervisor could treat you just like your mother did. A coworker could remind you of the way a sibling used to talk to you.

Cindy was already seeing me for depression when another problem cropped up. Work had been one of the few places Cindy felt good about herself. Her home life might be a disaster, but at work Cindy felt like she knew what she was doing. But lately the thought of going to work sent her into a panic.

As I reviewed her work situation, Cindy explained that although she was doing the same job, she had a new supervisor. The previous one had been a friendly, laid-back man who enjoyed jokes and gave Cindy a high degree of freedom to do her job without interference. Her new supervisor was completely different. Rarely smiling, he seemed to Cindy to hover over her desk, alert for anything she might be doing wrong. It wasn't just her; he was like that with the other women in her department.

Soon after he'd begun work over her section, an accounting error had been found. Not a major one, but enough to raise eyebrows. Everyone was understandably nervous about tracking the cause of the error. To Cindy's horror, one of her coworkers intimated to the new supervisor that Cindy was responsible. Instead of asking her about it, he immediately assumed she was at fault. Though the error couldn't be traced back to her, he now treated her as if her work product was inferior to the others. Not only was she working under a suspicious boss, but she'd found out just what kind of a friend she had in her coworker.

This would have been a difficult situation for anyone. But as we talked about it, Cindy said to me, "You know, I felt just like when my dad used to get mad at us. I was always the one to blame. I could never do anything right. And Mom used to let Dad think that I was at fault. She never stood up for me. I was the scapegoat.

"That's just how I felt at work when that happened. Like I was a kid again. My boss was my dad and my friend was my mom. There I was again, taking the blame for something I didn't do!"

Cindy was able to confront her friend about how she had acted and learn to work for her boss without feeling guilty about doing her job. She had to pull herself away from her past patterns and deal with her work situation in the present. It wasn't long before her boss was transferred to another department where he wasn't responsible for the work product of so many employees.

Our family relationships are the foundation for how we interact with people in the future. If the foundation is shaky, it needs to be shored up with healthy models of positive relationships.

No amount of money is worth staying in an abusive working environment. There are laws now to protect workers from what is known as a hostile work environment as it relates to outright harassment. If you find yourself in a hostile work environment with an abusive person, you should consider looking for another job, even if the law isn't on your side. Is it fair that you should have to leave your job? No. But it might be better for you in the long run.

Your Spiritual Relationship

Whatever your religious background, you probably have come into contact with the concept of God being a higher authority. Often the person in your past who abused you was in a position of authority over you—an adult or an older child. Because of that abuse, it is natural to develop a fear of authority in any form, including spiritual authority. A response to this fear of authority can take two paths. One is to completely reject authority of all kinds, especially spiritual. The other is to wholeheartedly embrace an adult equivalent to the oppressive authority you experienced as a child.

If your response has been to reject all authority, you have probably sworn off religion. After all, religious faith recognizes God's authority as higher than your own, and involves conforming your life and actions to his will. If you grew up in a rigid, overbearing relationship with someone in authority, conforming yourself to anyone's will again might be extremely difficult. You may not have had any choice about being under the abusive authority you suffered in the past, but you sure have a say now! And there's no way you're going to get involved with any kind of church with all their rules and regulations! Religion is simply not for you.

The other response is to seek within religion the kind of tight, consuming control you experienced as a child. Often this is the reason many people willingly give up their freedom of choice and join cults, even those destructive cults that ultimately have led to the tragic deaths of the followers, such as at Jonestown or Waco. In a cult there is usually a charismatic central figure who is alternately regarded as a god to his or her followers and as a father or mother figure. This type of personality attracts those who are seeking the comfort of a controlling personality who will tell them what to do and give their life meaning.

Whether the response is to reject all religious authority or seek a controlling cult group, the ability to have healthy spiritual relationships is hindered because of emotional abuse. Our relationships should support us and give us a sense of belonging and unity. Spiritual relationships can do that in a way that few other relationships can, but only if they are healthy. Spiritual relationships that merely repeat the patterns of past abuse are not fulfilling their proper function. If you have been frustrated in developing your own spiritual relationship, look to your past relationships for evidence of abuse. Find someone to help you stop repeating the same unhealthy patterns in the one relationship you need most.

Relationship with Children

I have saved this relationship for last because it can be the most difficult to deal with. Not that children are the most difficult to deal with, but because if you are a parent, so much of your very self can be tied up in your children.

"Mommy, I hurt myself!" Jessica's youngest ran up to her, tears streaming. Dropping everything, Jessica scooped him up in her arms and comforted him. Two seconds before he had been trying to get her attention, but she was putting away groceries and had been busy. But now he was hurt, and all her attention was focused on him.

Jessica grew up in a nonaffectionate household. No one had ever been there to hold her when she fell or scraped a knee. Now when one of her kids was hurt, she made sure they were treated better than she had been.

What started out as wonderful when they were little soon turned into a problem as they got older. Whenever any of them wanted attention, they simply "got hurt." If Mommy was too busy, too preoccupied with one of the other children, with Daddy, or talking on the phone, a finger or toe would get hurt, a knee would get bumped, or one of a hundred other small complaints would loudly be proclaimed to ensure that Mommy stopped whatever she was doing and listened to them.

Eventually it was all Jessica could do to work on one thing for any length of time without being interrupted. Frustrated at all the crying and complaints, she began to respond in anger.

"Why can't you kids leave me alone for just five minutes?! I can never get anything done around here without one of you coming up and whining about something!"

She'd rant and rave for a second or two, but the kids knew nothing would ever come of it. Jessica had trouble disciplining her children. Every time she thought of it, she'd remember what it was like growing up. Though she knew her children needed her to set boundaries and limits on their behavior, she couldn't seem to get past her negative reaction to those limits. As a consequence, Jessica found herself losing control of her children. They began to control her. And when they did, she generally lost control of her anger.

It was a vicious cycle that needed to be stopped.

Unfortunately, abuse of all kinds is a vicious cycle that keeps going 'round and 'round, from generation to generation. Part of the cyclical nature of abuse is to enter into abusive relationships in the future because of past ones. Within those abusive relationships it is possible for the abused to become the abuser, repeating the pattern of abuse learned at the hands of his or her abuser.

So much research points to the fact that abusers in our society today were themselves abused as children. Many of you who were emotionally abused in the past may find yourself acting out the abuse you suffered onto those around you. Children have always been a convenient target for that abuse.

Emotional abuse can have a devastating effect on all personal relationships. That is why it is so vital if you have been emotionally abused that you acknowledge the fact of that abuse, no matter how painful the realization, and actively learn how to overcome the effects of that abuse.

Part Four

Overcoming Emotional Abuse

10

Recognizing Your Abuse and Its Effects

There comes a critical time in each person's life when the truth is accessible. Faced with it, you can either run and hide, denying it, or you can face your truth and accept it. Truth doesn't stop being truth because we refuse to look at it. It simply remains an unacknowledged truth that hangs around our necks like an albatross. Far too many of us go through life trying numerous destructive ways to deny our truth. Now is the time to stop. Now is the time to face your truth.

While reading this book, you have been presented with many different ideas and a lot of information about emotional abuse. You've been able to see the effect it has had in the lives of some of the people with whom I have come into contact. In looking back and reviewing what you've read so far, it's time to shift from a *them* mode to a *me* mode. As you read this chapter, meditate on how it applies to you directly.

Ignoring, Denying, Accepting, Perpetuating

Previous chapters have shown why it has been so hard in the past to recognize your abuse for what it is. You have seen that your life pattern, your family, your society, and even your historical culture have all conspired to mask over the terrible truth about the effects of emotional abuse. You have seen the way you have been conditioned to ignore the emotional abuse around you. Its sheer prevalence inundates your senses, forcing you to relegate it to the position of background noise in your life.

When you could no longer ignore its existence, you learned to deny its ill effects. You went out of your way to justify your abusers, convincing yourself they had a right to treat you the way they did. Numbing the pain, you stubbornly clung to the illusion that "sticks and stones may break my bones, but words will never hurt me!"

However, ignoring it didn't work, and denying its damage was sometimes impossible, so you learned to accept it as a part of your life—unchangeable. It became a fact of life— something that had to be dealt with stoically and survived with the minimal amount of pain possible.

Finally, because you tried to ignore it, sought to deny it, and learned to accept it as a normal part of life, you were left with nothing else but to perpetuate it and its effects in your own life and relationships.

You should not beat yourself up because you didn't see it sooner. There are valid reasons why recognizing your abuse was extremely difficult. Instead, you should be applauding your vision, your ability to see through all of the smoke screens sent up by these powerful influences. You have seen through to the truth about emotional abuse in general and are ready to accept the truth of your own abuse in particular.

Recognizing Your Emotional Damage

As you begin to take a hard look at your own personal history of abuse and abusive relationships, there will be a natural tendency to want to minimize the horror of what has happened to you. This is a very natural reaction. Reluctant to relive the pain, your mind will try to convince you that what you remember wasn't so bad.

It is important at this time to take a moment and remind yourself just how damaging emotional abuse really is. You will be fighting against the repeated, implanted messages that were programmed into you by those who abused you and by society at large. You must fight those messages by accepting the truth of the pain you feel.

Remember, also, how damaging the emotions are that emotional abuse triggers: fear, guilt, and anger. Other damaging emotions caused by emotional abuse fall under these main categories. Think back to how it felt for you when you were in the midst of being abused, how you felt after the abuse was over, and how much you feared for the abuse to start all over again. When the messages from the past try to tell you you're "making a mountain out of a mole hill," remember the feelings you had while toiling up that "mole hill."

Recognizing the Abuser

At this point it would be helpful to go over again the specific types of abusers talked about in chapters 4 through 6. As you read through them again, think about those you have had contact with in the past or present who fit each mold. These are individuals you will need to be very careful in dealing with in the future, even avoiding them if necessary. They have the potential to become toxic people in your life.

Emotional Abuse through Words

The Overbearing Opinion—Another person refuses to consider your opinion and forces you to always accept his or hers.

The Person Who Is Always Right—Whenever there is a disagreement of any sort, this person always has to be right and have the last say.

The Judge and Jury—The person who incorporates harsh judgments of you as a person or your behavior as a way to produce personal shame and guilt.

The Put-Down Artist—The person who uses comments like "You're crazy! How could anyone think such a stupid thing?" to devalue your decisions and feelings.

The Stand-Up Comic—The person whose use of sarcasm is meant to dig up past issues, drive home a point of view, or belittle you as an individual.

The Great Guilt-Giver—This person uses unrealistic and undeserved false guilt to control your behavior.

The Historian—The person who tells you you're forgiven but then proceeds to bring up over and over again every past issue to shame you into accepting his or her decisions and feelings.

Emotional Abuse through Actions

The Commander-in-Chief—The person who desires to control every aspect of your life from your thoughts to your actions by rigid, militaristic behavior and expectations.

The Screamer—This is the person who uses screaming, yelling, and name-calling as weapons to control you.

The Intimidator—Intimidation, fear, anger, and inappropriate threats are used by this person to get his or her way.

The Roller Coaster—This person's moods and behavior swing from one extreme to another, removing any sense of safety and consistency from your relationship.

The Dr. Jekyll and Mr. Hyde—There is a public persona and a private persona that are distinctly different from each other, with the public person using a false front to mask his or her true nature.

The Person Who Plays Favorites—This person displays the "Why can't you be more like . . . ?" favoritism, making it clear that you do not measure up to the other child.

The Role Reverser—Relational roles become confused and reversed, with the parent taking the role of child, the child assuming the responsibilities of the parent, or the child being put in the role of the emotional spouse.

The Wrath of God—The person who misuses Scripture to get his or her own way and who equates his or her own opinion with that of God.

Emotional Abuse through Indifference

The M.I.A. Parent—A parent *physically* removes himself or herself from any interaction in your life.

The Absent Caregiver—A parent removes himself or herself *emotionally* from interaction in your life.

By this time you have probably already identified who these people are. As you have read over the examples, you have probably also relived some of the emotions you felt being associated with these people. It would be easier at this point to say everything has been done, that as long as you've identified your abusers, you are now free to go on with your life, vowing never to have anything to do with them again. But recognizing your abusers is only the beginning step to recognizing the long-term effects of their abuse.

Recognizing the Effect on You

Because your abuse was part of your past, it has contaminated your present self. You must deal with yourself and the effect your abuse has on past, present, and future relationships. In chapter 7 I discussed the ways I've seen abuse affect people I've worked with. Take some time to think them over again. Discover whether you feel you have been affected in ways I haven't mentioned. Each person is unique. While the effects can be similar, they need not be identical.

Low self-esteem
Lack of self-confidence
Transfer of needs
Perfectionism
Inappropriate relationships
Failure syndrome
Unrealistic guilt
Crisis oriented
Unresolved anger and resentments

I'm sure you can add one or more of your own after thinking about that list. Just because something common to you isn't up there, that doesn't mean the effect isn't valid. These are presented to you as guidelines, as frameworks within which you can explore the effects of your abuse as it applies uniquely to you.

Recognizing the Effects on Your Health

Your emotions don't operate within a vacuum. The emotional delivery system is chemical and body-based. What your mind feels, your body experiences.

Over the years you may have developed chronic health problems that seem impervious to medical treatment. Doctors may have shaken their heads and muttered under their breath that they could find nothing wrong with you. In reviewing the list of physical reactions I gave in chapter 8, think about your own state of health and how the emotional abuse in your past may have contributed to ongoing physical conditions you are facing now.

Addictions
Allergies/asthma
Depression
Digestive disturbances
Eating disorders
Free-floating anxiety
Hypochondria
Migraine headaches
Panic attacks
Phobias
Unexplained skin rashes

In no way am I trying to say that every physical problem you may currently be facing is a direct result of the emotional abuse you've suffered. However, if you have hard-to-explain, chronic problems that have defied treatment, maybe it's time to look for more than just an organic source.

Recognizing the Effects of Negative Messages

Past negative messages can affect you in several different ways. Those messages of failure and inadequacy may cause you to never attempt to do or achieve anything. You may have developed a dependency on others to carry out routine tasks. The very thought of attempting to achieve something noteworthy or special may cause an immediate panic reaction of *What am I even thinking of? I could never do that!* And so, of course, you don't. The fear of failure is so great that you become paralyzed and achieve very little, further substantiating the messages that say, "You're nothing."

The opposite reaction of doing nothing is attempting to do everything. I have found that most often the tendency toward perfection is driven by a series of messages given to an individual that "motivate" their desire to be perfect. Stated and implied messages like "You're not good enough, thin enough, smart enough, strong enough . . ." are replayed over and over in the back of your mind. They can warp your view of yourself, sap emotional energy, and drive you to constantly prove those messages wrong by engaging in superhuman feats of effort and stamina.

In order to determine what those messages are, you need to first evaluate how you feel about yourself. Emotional abuse tears at a person's sense of self-worth. The verbal and non-verbal messages conveyed through emotional abuse are like tapes that are played over and over in our minds. "I'm not worth anything," or "I'll never be able to do that," aren't generally assumptions we've come to on our own. We've been "helped" along the way by the opinions of others, transferred to us through their words and actions.

Take a moment and get out a piece of paper. Fold the paper in half lengthwise. On one side write down how you feel about yourself—what sort of person you are, what your goals are for yourself. Try to use single words or phrases to describe what you think of yourself.

Looking at each characteristic or description of yourself, think about when you first came to feel that way. Is this an opinion you came to on your own? Did you hear or feel it from someone else? Who? Write down the origin of your opinion. (Also write down the first thoughts that come to mind. Don't talk yourself out of whatever your answer is. No matter how odd or far-fetched your recollection seems, go ahead and write it down.)

Look back over what you have written. How many positive characteristics or goals do you have? How many negative? The more perfectionistic you are, the more negatives will occur on your list. While the normal person will be able to see both their good and bad qualities, the person who has suffered emotional abuse will often see an overbalance of negative traits.

As you identify these negative messages and where they came from, you can begin to erase them from the tape recorder that is your subconscious mind. You erase them by seeing them for what they are and by identifying their origin. Many of them have to do with who you were, not who you are. As we grow up, we change and make progress in our thinking and behaviors. As we pass from childhood into adulthood, we may need to reevaluate those messages and hear them as the adults we are, not as the children we were.

But often it is not enough just to erase the old messages; they have the ability to come back when least expected or desired. In order to ensure that negative messages are permanently erased, it will be necessary to record over them with positive messages of self-worth and acceptance. It is important that these messages come first from you.

There are a variety of ways to fill your life with positive messages about yourself. Place "You Are Special!" magnets or stickers where you will see them often (refrigerator, work desk, bedroom or bathroom mirror). Reward yourself on a regular basis with some thing that you've decided reinforces your worthiness (fresh flowers on your desk, a new haircut, a routine walk in the park). At first this might seem awkward or contrived; that's because it is. The messages in your mind are like whispers of background noise. Sometimes you'll need to drown them out with something you can see, hear, or touch. Whenever you see it or do it you'll be reminded that you are a special person.

Another way to record positive messages is through the appreciation of other people. Try joining a service club or church. Focusing on others and helping them can give a needed break and new perspective on our own problems. And besides, service groups are notorious for needing help! They are often highly appreciative of those who take the time to volunteer. If you are hesitant to try something new, remember that most groups will extend extra patience for anyone willing to volunteer time and energy. Let their appreciation for your efforts help record over some of your negative messages!

Another important way to build up your self-esteem and tear down those negative messages is to surround yourself with positive people. Of course, the first person to surround yourself with is . . . you. Make a conscious effort to be positive and encouraging, and to forgive yourself. Then look for others who make you feel good about yourself, who appreciate you for who you are.

Since nobody is perfect, the negative messages will resurface from time to time, probably when you're under a stressful situation. This is normal. They were recorded under stressful situations, and those are the times that are most likely to bring them out. So don't be surprised, be prepared. Be prepared to put your present stressful situation into perspective without bringing up the tapes of the past. Turn up those positive messages FULL BLAST!

Recognizing the Effects on Relationships

As we have seen, perhaps one of the most important truths for you to recognize if you've been emotionally abused is that in most cases your abuse will have adversely affected the way you view yourself. It will be necessary to go back through your mind and replay those negative messages associated with your abuse, realize they were false messages, and start rerecording positive, uplifting, life-changing messages of your own.

In addition, if you are in a long-term or permanent relationship with another person, you will need to ascertain just how your relationship is being adversely affected by your abuse and your past and present response to that abuse.

In chapter 9 I reviewed several of the difficulties in relationships that I have seen in working with those who have been emotionally abused. An honest evaluation of whether emotional abuse has hindered past relationships, is hindering present relationships, or might hinder future relationships is necessary to being able to develop and maintain the kind of healthy interaction so necessary to communication and growth in relationships.

One of those problems may be in experiencing and maintaining a necessary sense of intimacy with your sexual partner. It is difficult to totally relax around another person if we are constantly on guard.

Overcoming a fear of sexual intimacy will take time and patience. Identifying why being with another person is frightening or uncomfortable for you is essential. If your partner is willing to discuss such a sensitive subject with you, you can talk together about your sexual experiences and how you feel about them. Initially, it would be helpful if these discussions could stand on their own, without the expectation that they will lead to sexual intimacy. Without the pressure to perform, you may both be able to relax and be more open about how you feel.

Sometimes it is good, when dealing with such a charged subject, to obtain professional help. Talking to a third party or having a third party present can help diffuse tension. A counselor or health professional can also be helpful in knowing which questions to ask and in providing physical or anatomical information that you may not have access to.

As your acceptance of yourself grows, as you rerecord positive messages about yourself, as you learn to relax around yourself and enjoy who you are, your ability to relax around others will increase. Much of the fulfillment of sexual intimacy has to do with relaxing and enjoying yourself, your partner, and the experience itself.

Included within the resource list at the back of this book are other books that can aid you in your search for deeper sexual intimacy.

Another thing that may contaminate your current relationships is the desire for perfectionism. Letting go of your own need to be perfect will allow you to release the rigid control over your environment and those in it. Understand that it is normal and realistic for people, even yourself, to make mistakes. Be gentle and forgiving with yourself when you fall short. Remember the positive things about yourself. Learn to laugh at your mistakes and move on.

Again, it all has to do with a sense of perspective. No one is perfect. No one can be perfect. All we can do is our best, whatever that means for each person. Each of us needs to be given a break, to be allowed to be human.

When we are happy with ourselves and at ease with where we are and where we're going, then we can relax around others. We no longer see them as obstacles to our perfect goals that must be maneuvered around, or as walking, talking pawns to be moved at our will on the chessboard of our lives.

Anger, fear, and guilt are powerful emotions. If you were abused as a child, these emotions were an essential part of growing up. Your abuse intensified them, and you were left with no healthy model of how to cope with these emotions. You will need to recognize the ways in which you are still trying to deal with the anger, fear, and guilt left over from your abusive relationships.

Any part of your body that gets hit over and over again becomes sensitive. Even though a callus might form, there will still be immediate and intense pain if it is hit in the right spot. Within relationships, your abuse has left you with several sensitive spots. If they are touched, even if not by the person who did most of the damage, it will still hurt you. When you are hurt, you may react with anger, fear, or feelings of guilt. You may explode in anger one day over some inconsequential incident. The person who set you off might not even understand what he or she has done, and certainly not why you're acting in such an odd way.

A casual comment at work could lead you to fear whether your employer or coworker likes you or thinks you're doing a good job. Or the same comment could cause you to negatively reevaluate your work performance and feel guilty for some "error" on your part.

Again, you need to gain a sense of perspective and try to identify why what was done produced such a reaction. If possible, try to remember other times in your life when you felt the same way. Determine whether the anger, fear, or guilt you feel is really related to the current situation or is a holdover from some past incident.

Everyone will blow up in anger over something little—whether it's the guy that cut you off on the freeway, the busy signal you always seem to get when you call that number, or the fact the waitress gave you cream in your coffee instead of leaving it black. Pile up enough of those annoyances, and most people will need to let off steam. But if the explosion of steam is wildly out of proportion, or if you find the anger, fear, or guilt doesn't subside as quickly as it came, then it's time to find yourself a quiet place and think about why you're feeling the way you are. If you can't come up with an answer or if this seems to happen too often, it would be very helpful to find someone to talk with. It doesn't necessarily have to be a professional; just a friend will often do.

If you hold down a job outside your home you will by necessity develop relationships at work. They are not immune to the effects of your abuse. Emotional abuse can damage all your relationships. Be aware of feeling inadequate on the job, of feeling that somehow the good things that are happening in your career are undeserved, or of looking at your work relationships through the lens of familial ones where a boss becomes father, a supervisor becomes mother, or a coworker becomes sibling. When this situation arises, you have a couple of choices. The obvious one is to find another job. However, that may not solve the problem. You may find yourself feeling the same way in another position with another person.

The other choice is to stay where you're at and deal with the way you feel about this person. Try doing what I call a reality check. If your employer calls you into his office to talk about something, say to yourself before you open the door, "He is not my father. He's just my boss." If your supervisor criticizes some piece of work, remind yourself after she's left, "She is not my mother, and I am not a child any more." If a coworker begins to expect you to do too many favors or cover for him at work, tell yourself, "We are both employees. He is not my brother, and I don't need to make up excuses for him. It's not fair to myself or my employer."

Maintaining a sense of present-day reality on the job can go a long way in helping you deal with individuals whose personalities seem to correspond with past relationships. Getting to know whoever you're having a problem relating to can also help solidify that person's own identity in your mind. The better you know them, the less like someone else they may seem.

Finally, when looking at your relationships, don't forget your spiritual nature. This is an important aspect of your whole person. Your relationship with God can help you define who you are, why you are here, and where you are going. If you have a tendency to view God as a stern, unforgiving superparent, the relationship you have with him will be nothing more than an enlarged copy of your relationship with the parent who abused you. Your spiritual relationship should offer you comfort, peace, and security, not a supernaturally motivated repeat of anger, fear, and guilt.

In order to change the perception of God as unforgiving, you could start with two things. First, try reading the Bible. It's amazing how many people who profess to follow it haven't actually read it for themselves! This time, read it without any one else telling you what God says or God demands. Allow God to reveal himself through his words to you personally, unfiltered by another's perspective or bias. Seek to develop your own relationship with him. Let him speak to you directly, not through someone else. Try underlining all the places where his grace, mercy, and forgiveness are shown or promised.

Second, observe the people around you in your religious setting. If they, for the most part, reinforce this vision of the stern, unforgiving God, it might be wise to seek out another group. There are many churches and religious groups in this country. Seek out one where God's grace and forgiveness are emphasized. Before you become fully involved in a religious body, set up an appointment with one of the leaders and find out how they view God. If it's too much like the harsh view you grew up with, seek somewhere else, with God's help.

Recognizing Your Abuse through Your Children

Nothing seems to put people into better contact with their parents than becoming a parent themselves. If your abuser was either your mother or your father, becoming a parent yourself will undoubtedly bring up the memory of that past abuse. Either you will attempt to scrupulously avoid any hint of abuse, swinging to the side of overprotectionism, or you may find yourself coming full circle by abusing your own children as you were abused. This is one of the most difficult truths you will have to face. Please don't turn away from it. There is too much at stake.

Because so much is involved, I cannot urge you enough to immediately seek professional counseling for this situation. This is a time when I say, don't walk—*run*—to the nearest help. In most places there are county or government programs that are either free or on a sliding fee scale if financial resources are a problem. Both you, your children, and your entire family can benefit greatly from professional help.

The time is now to stand up and say, "I'm going to put an end to this cycle of abuse. I need help to deal with my own abuse and I need help to not be an abuser myself." With a professional to guide you, you can work towards a healthy parenting style. One that neither overdisciplines with harshness and abuse, nor underdisciplines by failing to provide needed boundaries for the child. With proper guidance, your family can find a healthy, happy medium. It's what you so desperately needed and wanted as a child. Now it's time to give that to your own children and to yourself.

Recognizing Your Whole Person

You are a person who is connected to others through a web of personal and spiritual relationships. Emotional, physical, spiritual, relational—your whole person. To deny one aspect of yourself is to blind yourself to the interdependency of these different aspects. The effects of emotional abuse can damage all of these areas. Healing only part of your whole person still leaves part that is wounded.

Healing the whole person is possible. It happens when you get over the past and start living for the future. Now is the time to face up to your truth and begin.

11

Getting Over
the Past
and Living
for the Future

Of all of the chapters in this book, this is one I have longed to share since I began writing. This is where I tell you there is hope—that healing is possible! This is definitely the good news. Granted, it will take courage to heal. But having courage to face these difficult issues will result in hope. Hope opens up the heart to change. Where change is present, healing can begin.

I have so wanted to let you know that it is possible to get over a past where you suffered abuse and begin to really live for the future. In this chapter we are going to talk about specific ways to help you do just that.

Much of the work to be done can only be accomplished by you, either by working alone, or with the guidance of a trained professional. If you have a friend who has the appropriate skills to help you, that's great. Use whichever situation feels most comfortable. Whatever it takes to get on with your life, do it.

Getting on with your life means putting those feelings of anger, fear, and guilt into perspective. In this chapter we'll talk about how to get beyond your anger by stepping out of the blame mode and learning how to grant forgiveness. We'll look into how to banish the fear and guilt you've been feeling and reclaim your personal power.

This chapter will also give you some practical solutions in how to handle future conflicts. You'll learn nine helpful steps you can use to combat negative emotions when someone hurts you. You'll discover ways to find and maintain proper relationships with others and learn the traits of a healthy communicator. I'll give you some characteristics of healthy problem-solvers. I also want you to start thinking about your own gifts and talents that you might have buried. Finally, I'll go over how to recognize progress in your own healing process.

Over the years I've learned there are several things that a person can do to help themselves along the healing process. In this chapter we'll discuss:

- How to step out of the blame mode so common in abuse
- How to grant forgiveness, and why forgiveness is vital to healing
- How to reclaim your personal power
- How commonsense solutions can help avoid future conflicts
- Ten steps to take when someone hurts you
- How to find and maintain healthy relationships
- Traits of a healthy communicator
- How to discover your own gifts and talents
- Characteristics of a healthy problem-solver
- How to recognize progress in your own healing

Stepping Out of the Blame Mode

After years of living with false guilt, fear, and repressed anger, it is common to unleash a torrent of rage and regret at what has happened to you. The tears of anger and sorrow intermix as the truth is faced. After all that has been said and done to deny the truth of your abuse, when it finally is faced, it hurts. The fresh pain produces even more anger.

Anger can be a cleansing emotion. It is focused and intense. It has a way of motivating normally unwanted actions. When we are angry, we are apt to do things we would never consider doing otherwise. Anger is powerful. It can make us feel strong and invincible.

Because anger is so focused, its beam is narrow.
Because anger is so intense, it needs fuel to burn.
Because anger is so powerful, it can become addictive.

When dealing with your emotional abuse, it may be easy to view things with tunnel vision. All you may see is the pain and damage of the abuse. You may not see some of the reasons behind it. Nothing can explain it away.

Some people have the distinct misfortune of coming into contact with truly evil people who abuse them in terrible ways. Most of the rest of you have been abused by people who meant better than what they did, who tried less than what they should, who should have known better but didn't.

If you were abused by your parent, one reason behind the abuse may very well be that your parent had been abused. Abuse breeds abuse in a cyclical nature. If you find yourself being abusive to other people, it should help you understand how your own abuse was possible.

However, being angry or engaging in blame over abuse you suffered or self-blame for abuse you are responsible for will only detract from your healing. Anger may have the power to cleanse, but continued anger blocks healing.

Maintaining your sense of outrage and resentment toward the unfairness of life and toward those who abused you keeps you in bondage to that blaming mode. The anger ceases to cleanse and starts to control. In order for the anger to continue, you must constantly feed the fire, reliving and reexperiencing the anger and rage, thus stoking the fires of blame.

As these fires are stoked, the flame burns red hot. Tall, leaping flames of rage erupt. You are ready to devour everything in your path. You feel powerful and in control, perhaps for the first time in your life. It feels good. You feel strong— so strong no one will ever try to hurt you again.

You can't maintain that fire without blame—blaming yourself for the abuse you've received; blaming yourself for the abuse you've given; blaming others for both. This fire of blame will consume you.

That is why it is so important for you to get out of the blame mode. You can do that by trying to understand your abuser. So often abuse occurs because of faulty parenting patterns, without malicious intent. Abuse can also happen when an adult simply forgets what it means to be a child, when the parent stops taking the time to view the world from three feet high.

Sometimes abuse occurs and it really has nothing to do with you—it just happens to you. The other person is tired, careless, stressed, distracted, moody, or any number of things. Every single one of us has felt this way and acted toward others in this way. Every single one of us is to blame for something.

Getting past the blame helps you get past the abuse and get on with your life. You get out of the blame mode by trying to understand what was really behind your abuse. Was the other person evil? If your abuser was truly evil, blaming him or her will have little negative effect on the abuser and a great negative effect on you. Constant blame will only allow the abuser to continue to hurt you more because it keeps you stuck in the abuse cycle.

Was the other person not evil but weak? So much abuse is done by people who really ought to know better but for some reason can't see what it is they are doing. Both abused and abuser can be caught in the trap of ignoring and denying, accepting and perpetuating. Blaming continues the cycle. Forgiveness ends it.

The Healing Power of Forgiveness

Emotional abusers seek to strip away your sense of control and security. In an obsessive need to control their surroundings, emotional abusers use inappropriate ways to ensure the compliance of those with whom they are in relationship. Their need to control is so great, they cannot tolerate anyone else retaining control over his or her own life. They feel as if they have no control, so they rip yours away and take it for themselves.

Forgiveness returns you to a state of being in control. No one can bestow your forgiveness on another person but you. You are in total control of your own power to forgive.

Forgiveness does not mean that you forget all that has happened to you. It still hurts. But living obsessed with the pain and determined to continue the blame only perpetuates the damage.

Forgiveness validates that there is something to forgive. By saying "I forgive," you forgive the situation even if you can't forgive the person. By saying "I forgive," the control is given back to you. Depending on your situation, you may or may not be able to forgive your abuser face-to-face.

If you are the abuser, you can forgive yourself face-to-face. You can look at yourself and your situation. You can read your own heart and acknowledge your own desire to change and grow.

If your abuser is out of your life, you can attempt to contact that person through a phone call, letter, or visit. However, it is important to realize that it may not be physically possible for you to be in the same place as your abuser. If the abuser still has a powerful effect on you, any contact you have could be damaging and should be avoided until you're strong enough.

It is also possible that your abuser has come to understand the damage he or she has caused and may have already come to you seeking forgiveness. If that is the case, the gift of forgiveness you give will be a blessing for you both.

If your abuser is dead, you can still forgive. The person may no longer be alive to receive your forgiveness, but you can still grant it. Although the abuser can no longer be affected by what you do, your forgiveness can affect you. Remember, the most important person that forgiveness is going to help is you. Forgiving allows you to go on with your life. If you are able to forgive face-to-face, you should do so, but it is not necessary to actually be with the person for you to forgive.

If the abuser is in denial over the abusive behavior, he or she won't accept your forgiveness. Even your granting forgiveness will most likely be met with abuse and hostility. In cases such as these, a letter or a short, to-the-point phone call would be more appropriate than a physical confrontation.

When in doubt, start with something safe, like a letter. Put your forgiveness down on paper where you're able to choose your words in the safety of your own home. Depending how your letter is received you can determine whether to follow-up with another letter, phone call, or actual visit.

There is no set way to deliver the forgiveness. Whatever the method, you must determine in your own mind that you are going to forgive. How you go about delivering that forgiveness is up to you. Your response and attitude toward your abuser is totally up to you. It is just one step in reclaiming your personal power.

Reclaiming Your Personal Power

For much of your life you were bombarded with words, actions, and ideas that were designed to make you think you were powerless. It's time to change that.

You have worth and value. You have rights and power that should never have been taken from you. You have the right not to be verbally abused. You have the power to say "No!" if someone else tries to hurt you. You have the right to get on with your life and put your past behind you. You have the power to start the process of healing.

Even by reading this book you are saying to yourself that you believe you have the power to change. The messages of your abuse can be recorded over by relearning and reclaiming your sense of self. It is high time you found out about the real you.

If you are still in an abusive relationship, it will be difficult but not impossible for you to reclaim your personal power. But doing so will be confrontive to the person who is so aggressively trying to rob you of it. You may find it necessary to remove yourself from relationship with this abusive person while you change or until he or she changes.

You need to reclaim the right to make your own decisions, even if they differ from the decisions of others. Remind yourself daily that you are an intelligent, responsible individual who has the capacity to direct the course of your own life. If you feel the need to gain wisdom and guidance in finding your true self, seek out a trusted friend or, if you are able, a trained professional. Only choose a person you feel safe with!

Start small as you learn to use your personal power. Perhaps you might begin by reorganizing your physical space— your house or apartment. Is it really the way you want it to be? Or has someone else unduly influenced your choices? What about your wardrobe? Are those really the clothes you like to wear? Or is that recorder in your head doing your shopping for you? How about the job you're at? Is that really what you want to be doing? How about the realtionship you're in?

Since each individual is different, your responses will be different as well. What will be common though, is beginning to have a say in your environment, the people who are around you, and how you are treated by those people.

Reclaiming your personal power will mean learning to say yes to yourself when needed and say no to others when warranted.

Use Common Sense to Avoid Conflicts

The greatest common sense you can use is to get out of an abusive situation if you see no immediate hope of change. This does not mean you must sever the relationship completely, but it may be necessary to put it on hold for a while. Abusive people are toxic people. They poison the relationships they are in through their attitudes and actions. In order to heal, you must first detoxify yourself by limiting contact with abusive individuals.

If you must maintain a relationship with a current or former abuser, try never to meet him or her alone. If your abuser was a parent, take a friend, spouse, or sibling with you when you meet. Try meeting at a location other than the home (e.g., a restaurant or store), and bring someone else with you, explaining beforehand to this person that you need him or her to act as an emotional shield for you. When no such person is available, it might be wise to avoid personal contact with your abuser.

An emotional shield is a person who can support you while you are confronting your abuser. It should be a close friend, sibling, or spouse; someone who pledges beforehand to act as a buffer between you and your abuser if you start getting into trouble. Often people are "private" abusers. They act differently around others than they do when they feel safe and private. Just by bringing another person with you, you may be able to diffuse some of those private patterns.

Every confrontation with an abuser will be different, but the following example may show you how you could use an emotional shield if you feel it necessary to physically meet with your abuser.

Jill decided it was finally time to confront her father. She dreaded the thought of doing it, but he continued to criticize every decision she made, even though she was married and hadn't lived under his roof for years. She wasn't sure if he would ever change, but she wanted to let him know that she had forgiven him for the way he'd treated her as a child. She wanted him to know she was no longer going to allow him to deal with her in such a harsh, judgmental way. She was nervous and scared, but also determined.

Her husband, Paul, agreed to go along even though he, at first, insisted it was a family issue between Jill and her father. But even he was becoming tired of his father-in-law's derisive comments about Jill. Because of their strained relationship, Paul and Jill rarely went to visit her father at all. When they did, Jill became a different person. She acted differently, spoke differently, even dressed differently. Jill needed Paul there to remind her father that she wasn't just his little girl any more.

They agreed to meet at a local restaurant, one that had private booths and soft lighting. Jill knew her father would have to listen to her without yelling or risk public embarrassment. Of course, he could always walk out once he'd heard what she had to say, but that was a risk she was willing to take. She just couldn't put up with his behavior any longer. Since she didn't really want to cut all ties with him, this seemed the only way to deal with the problem.

It was awkward at first when they all met at the restaurant and waited in the lobby for their table. Her father knew she wanted to talk to him about something, but neither of them wanted to bring it up with a handful of strangers rubbing elbows with them.

They spoke of trivial things—the weather, the local sports teams. When the conversation drifted into how their daughter was doing in school, Jill felt the old tension coming back. With great relief, she heard their name being called for a table.

"Dad," Jill began after they'd ordered. "You know I'll always love you." It was her father's turn to be uncomfortable. He shifted in his seat and glanced around at Paul. "Sure, honey," he said quietly.

"But Dad, I've come to a decision about things. I just hope you'll understand." He looked puzzled but didn't respond.

"All my life," Jill continued, "it has seemed to me that you were never happy with anything I did." At this point, he tried to interrupt, to deny what she was saying. But Jill persisted.

"Please, Dad, let me finish. My grades were never good enough in school. You didn't like the clothes I wore or the friends I made. I've always wanted you to approve of me, but every time we talk there always seems to be something I should be doing that I haven't or something I did that I shouldn't.

"Dad, I've spent my whole life wanting you to, just once, listen to what I had to say or watch what I was doing without bringing up everything you thought was wrong.

"I want you to let go of me, Dad. I want you to let me be who I am without interfering or criticizing."

"Why are you saying this?" her father asked, ashen-faced and embarrassed. "If I thought you were doing wrong, it was my job as a parent to say so! What was I supposed to do? Let you go off and do something stupid and get hurt? I wouldn't be a very good parent if I let you do that!"

"But Dad," Jill said, taking a deep breath, "You never seemed to think anything I did was right. You could always find something wrong."

"Well, did you ever think it was because something *was* wrong? You pulled some pretty crazy stunts growing up! Come to think if it, this is a pretty crazy stunt. Is this what you brought me here to tell me, that I'm a bad father?" His voice had increased to a level just below shouting. Jill's eyes were beginning to flood with tears. Paul decided now was the time to speak up.

"Look, Bob," he began. "Nobody's saying you were a bad father. All Jill is asking you to do is think about how you treated her then and how you treat her now."

"I think this is between my daughter and me!"

"She's your daughter, but she's my wife and a mother herself. This affects all of us. We're just asking that you think about the way you speak to her and treat her."

"Dad, I'm not saying you meant to be mean or cruel, all I know is how you've made me feel. I still desperately want you to approve of me, but I can't spend the rest of my life trying to get something you're never going to give!"

No one spoke for a moment while their dinner was brought to the table. Slowly, her father began again in a quieter tone. "I was always so worried," he said, "that you'd hurt yourself and that it would be my fault. That I didn't teach you well enough how to ride a bike or climb a tree. That I didn't give you the skills you needed to choose your friends or stay out of trouble. I never wanted you to get hurt . . ."

"But I did get hurt, Daddy," Jill told him softly. "You hurt me . . ."

Paul just let his wife and her father talk. He really didn't have to say any more, just be there. As her father sought to try to understand how Jill saw things that had happened in the past, Paul was able to provide a few examples he'd seen in the time they'd been married. But mostly he just kind of moved into the background, asserting himself only when the conversation seemed to be tilting out of balance.

There are other sorts of shielding you can use besides another person. Using the telephone is another way to buffer yourself if you need to remain in contact with an abuser. There are a variety of ways to shorten or terminate a conversation on the telephone. The lack of face-to-face contact and the physical distance between you can help you separate yourself from the conversation if necessary.

If the mere presence of this person causes you anxiety, but you just don't feel you can withdraw the relationship completely, try to carry on a long-distance relationship by mail. Often this is an excellent way to begin the process of learning more about the other person, which may allow you to feel comfortable enough to eventually confront him or her about the abusive behavior. It can also be a good test of the abuser's willingness to make necessary changes in his or her relationship with you.

Nine Steps when Someone Hurts You

Being able to put your past abuse into perspective doesn't mean you'll be immune from being hurt in the present. If you're around people for very long, you'll end up being hurt by someone! Your past patterns of dealing with being hurt are not those you want to continue. So here are some steps you can take to deal with these current situations. They will help you to develop some new techniques and keep you from reacting to new hurts in old ways.

1. Recognize the offense for what it is. Is it intentional? Is it unintentional? Is it a misunderstanding? Listen to what your heart tells you about what happened. Usually your gut reaction is a good indicator of what you really think.

    It may be helpful to write out just what was said. It will often look different to you on paper. You may also want to write out how you felt about what happened.

You can use this to determine what you are going to do about it.

2. Resist the tendency to defend your position. If you determine that you need to confront the person who has hurt you, offer only your point of view about the incident.

3. Give up the need to be right. This can be an unfortunate leftover from your past abuse and can escalate a bad situation into a worse one.

4. Recognize and apologize for anything you might have done to contribute to the situation. Make certain, however, that it is a legitimate wrong or oversight and not false guilt brought on by past abuse.

5. Respond vs. react—learn to be proactive. This will require you to pause long enough to take the opportunity to think and evaluate. Sometimes just waiting will add needed perspective. By responding and not just reacting, you exert control over your behavior.

6. Adopt an attitude of bridge building as opposed to attacking or retreating. A conciliatory attitude is much easier for everyone to deal with than a hostile, defensive one. Practice maintaining an attitude of love and acceptance. This doesn't mean you agree with the person who has hurt you and with what he has done, but rather that you have chosen to react to him and his actions in a certain, predetermined way.

7. Realize you may be the target of someone's anger but not the source of that anger. You may find yourself in the unenviable position of being the proverbial straw that broke someone else's back. Take responsibility only for your part. Avoid falling into the trap of accepting false guilt from others.

8. Create your personal limits. This is part of reclaiming your personal power. You have the right to define what your limits are and to insist they be respected.

You probably are aware of behaviors you've put up with in the past that really annoy you and have made you feel that you were being treated disrespectfully or unfairly. You have a right to let your objections be heard. It needn't be in an angry, vengeful way but rather in an assertive, positive way that says, "I respect who I am as a person, and I would like you to do the same."

9. Realize that even if someone has hurt you, it need not take away your personal happiness. Remember, you are in charge of your attitude and response. You can get over it and go on.

How to Find and Maintain Healthy Relationships

If you want to maintain a healthy relationship, you must first find one. A healthy relationship is one where each individual experiences positive, uplifting consequences from the relationship, where individual opinions and personalities are respected, and where trust is the cornerstone upon which the relationship is built. If you have had trouble in the past finding someone who desired that kind of relationship, don't give up! Keep looking! For each one of you out there looking one way, there is someone else looking back. Keep looking until you find each other.

When seeking a healthy relationship, be alert to signs of a possible abuser. Pay attention to how the other person speaks to you and about you. Make certain you avoid people who show signs of any of the abusive behaviors we discussed in chapters 4 through 6.

As you are looking at the other person, don't forget to keep an eye on yourself. Be aware of how you may be affected by your abuse and how it may cause heightened patterns of perfectionism and hypersensitivity in you. Not only must you find a person with whom you want a relationship, but he or she has to be able to maintain a relationship with you.

The most effective way of maintaining a healthy relationship is by becoming healthy yourself. Even though the process is painful, don't substitute working on a healthy relationship for your own self-healing.

Look around you at friends and acquaintances who have loving relationships. You will be able to tell by the things they say and the way they act around each other whether or not it is the type of relationship you want to model. When you feel comfortable, ask questions. Seek to gain insight from them as to how they met and why they are still together. Some of the wisest counsel you can receive is from couples who have been together for many years. If your family pattern makes looking to grandparents suspect, seek out others in church, service groups, or social clubs.

The reading list at the end of this book suggests many fine books that deal with how to grow a healthy relationship. Take the time to read and reflect on the type of person you want to be individually and as part of a couple.

Most importantly, put what you learn into practice. Do not demand perfection, but keep on trying. This is part of learning to live differently than you have in the past. Once you have turned the corner away from abuse, just keep on going. Choosing to act differently can help keep you from turning back.

Up to now I've spoken about intimate relationships between couples, but many of these same rules apply for establishing and maintaining good friendships. Any time you open yourself to another person for a relationship, make sure you choose a person you can feel safe and comfortable with.

Traits of a Healthy Communicator

Since so much of emotional abuse is verbal and involved with how one person communicates with another, it is important to learn healthy communication in order to maintain a healthy relationship. As you communicate with those around you, remember these twelve guidelines:

1. Approach others with an attitude of gentleness and openness. Hostility closes down communication.
2. If you are attempting to solve a problem, avoid assuming a position of rightness before you even start. Your rightness implies all others are wrong. This could lead to a defensive attitude on their part.
3. Don't be afraid to speak the truth. Speak it confidently but without a desire to harm the other person.
4. Work on being able to separate how you feel about what you are saying from the message you are giving. It is important not to deny your emotions, but if you allow them free reign while you are communicating, your emotions can overshadow the message itself.
5. Be aware of the different ways men and women process information. Men and women often have differing worldviews—they may notice different details, or they may have different priority systems. This is not to be used as an excuse for unacceptable behavior, but it can help you to understand another person's perspective.
6. Allow the other person to hold an opinion that is different than yours.
7. Attempt to communicate an attitude of acceptance and love.
8. Make sure that your motivation to engage in the conversation is one of enhancing and improving the relationship as opposed to hurting the other person.
9. Allow the other person to make his or her own decisions.
10. Seek to inspire trust by extending understanding to the other person and by responding honestly to what is said.
11. Always make sure to seek forgiveness yourself when you make a mistake. Being able to admit your own failings will help the other person to feel comfortable enough to admit his or her own.
12. Be accountable for what you say you will do.

Maintaining communication within your relationships will require work, but the rewards will far outweigh your efforts.

Discover Your Gifts and Talents

You are unique. No one else is made quite like you. Each of us has a variety of talents and probably one true gift. Finding what your gifts and talents are can enhance your sense of self-worth. Practicing those gifts and talents will automatically add to your self-esteem.

A gift is usually defined as some activity you are exceptional at that requires no work on your part. You simply are able to do whatever it is with very little effort. It can be anything from public speaking to having a green thumb in the garden. Generally it is a thing that gives you great joy, and when you engage in it, you feel confident of yourself and what you are doing.

A talent, on the other hand, is something you are good at that requires practice. If you don't practice your talents, you tend to lose them. Often people choose one of their talents to use as their career. Doctors have a talent for medicine; accountants have a talent with numbers; bakers have a talent in the kitchen. Each has trained in his or her field and continues to maintain practice and hone his or her skills.

The negative messages from emotional abuse may have robbed you of the knowledge that you are special—that you are gifted and talented. By discovering your gifts and talents, you expose those messages for the lies they are.

If you are unsure of what your gifts and talents are, try remembering what you enjoyed doing as a child before other people stepped in to tell you what you were good at. Take a class at a community center or local college. Don't be afraid to take risks and try different things. There is no need to attain perfection in your gifts and talents, just to find out what they are. You may also want to read *Discovering Your God-Given Gifts,* by Don and Katie Fortune, listed in the reading list at the end of this book. Your gifts and talents should add to your quality of life and improve your sense of self-worth.

Characteristics of a Healthy Problem-Solver

Within any relationship you have, the time will come when a problem or conflict arises. Your past model of how to deal with that conflict will be faulty because of your abuse. Try these fifteen steps to work your way through to a solution:

1. Seek to resolve and deal successfully with the problem and not just be declared the winner.
2. Face your conflict instead of avoiding it.
3. Understand that different people can have different points of view concerning the problem and the best way to solve it.
4. Be clear about what is and is not acceptable in solving the problem. Do not accept abusive behavior of any kind.
5. Remember that people do make mistakes and have a need for forgiveness.
6. Take the initiative and forgive first.
7. Avoid the temptation to exact vengeance for any hurt inflicted.
8. Realize that there are times when the world is unfair, and sometimes you will be treated unfairly by others.
9. Approach the solution to the problem in a whole-person way: intellectually, emotionally, spiritually, and relationally.
10. Only attempt to solve one problem at a time. One is generally enough!
11. Anticipate a positive outcome to your problem-solving.
12. Be consistent in your effort to come to a resolution without trying to force a predetermined solution.

13. Understand the power you have to provide a solution through an understanding of who you are.
14. Search for commonsense solutions.
15. Be aware of verbal and nonverbal communication.

Healthy problem-solvers are better able to maintain supportive relationships through increased communication. Skill and improvement in this area can be used to improve other areas.

How to Recognize Progress

Finally, it is important for you to understand that getting over emotional abuse and living for the future is not a one-time revelation. Instead, it will be a healing process. Just as injuries and illnesses are seldom healed overnight, your emotional injuries will need time to heal.

This isn't a race you are trying to win. Avoid the perfectionist reaction of wanting to fix everything perfectly in as little time as possible—to show everyone and yourself how fast you can get over it.

The most any of us can ask for as we go through life is to grow toward being better people. Not perfect people, but better people—better toward ourselves, better toward our families, better toward the people we come into contact with each day. Doing so will not only bring about a more pleasant response from the people we meet, but it will also help us to feel good about ourselves.

Emotional abuse has been responsible for you feeling bad about yourself for too long. Now it's time to start feeling good! Now it's time to start knowing the wonderful person you really are!

It was ten o'clock in the morning, and Meg sat in her bathrobe drinking coffee. As she pulled deeply at her cigarette, she looked around and realized she hated everything about her life.

Her cluttered apartment. The stacks of unwashed dishes in the sink and on the counter with food drying to hardness.

Her job. The mindless, numbing repetition of inputting orders for hardware nails into an impersonal electronic box.

Her relationships. A boyfriend who never seemed to come home unless he was too drunk to be of much good. A mother she couldn't stand who kept calling on the phone to remind her what a mess she's made of her life.

Her looks. The twenty pounds overweight. All those lines and wrinkles that seemed to appear overnight.

Only twenty-seven years old, but she felt like fifty. Worse—she felt like her mother at fifty.

It seemed that somewhere along the line something had gone terribly wrong. This wasn't the life she thought she'd have. She remembered reading a beautiful book when she was four years old. It had big, bright pages with pictures of a sunny little house with happy smiling people on a long, tree-lined street. Oh, how she'd loved that book. She'd asked her daddy to read it over and over again. She'd memorized the pictures and would sit and dream about the kind of house she'd have when she grew up.

Twenty-three years later the book was long gone. And so was the dream. Her father had left the family after the birth of her brother when she was eight years old. He'd found someone he liked better than her mother. The last fight her parents had, her father had yelled at her mother so loudly she could hear him scream, "I just don't need you anymore!"

When she was eight, Meg was certain he was talking about her. At twenty-seven she wasn't so sure anymore, but still she hadn't spoken to him in years.

After her father left the family, times had been hard, and her mother had to get a job to support the family. Her mother was always tired at night, and Meg ended up taking on many of the household chores her mother simply did not have the energy to do. Her younger brother, Rob, never seemed to have to do as much as she did. He was the baby of the family, and Meg always knew her mother loved him more.

As soon as she could, Meg spent more and more time away from the house. She'd been pretty in high school, but that was before drinking too much had aged her body and clouds of cigarette smoke had yellowed her skin, hands, and teeth. Now she felt invisible. No one seemed to look at her with interest. Her current boyfriend only seemed to be interested in the money she brought home. Yes, back in high school she'd really been something to look at, with boys eager to be seen with her. But she always seemed to choose the hard-luck cases—the ones with problems at school or at home. She figured they were just like her.

Instead of going to college, Meg had gone to work right out of high school to help with the family bills. Her mother had developed a chronic back condition and was only drawing disability benefits. Meg had wanted to take up writing, but she ended up as a checker at the local mini-mart.

After seven years of standing on her feet all day, Meg had gotten the data entry job. At least now she could sit down. Of course, that's when the twenty pounds had come on.

Over the years she'd had several relationships—only one serious. Meg had wanted to get married, but he said he didn't want to be that tied down. Six months after she'd started pressing him on it, he left. The boyfriend she had now was a drunk, but at least he wouldn't leave her. His unemployment would run out soon, and where else was he going to get his beer money?

What ever happened to the bright, sunny house with the happy, smiling people on that long, tree-lined street? How in the world had that picture ever turned into the one Meg saw as she looked around? She sat the rest of the morning and all afternoon at the kitchen table, smoking, unable to move more than a few feet to the sink or the bathroom.

Come on, Meg! she said to herself as evening approached. *There's got to be more to life than this! That house is out there! There's got to be a way to find it!*

Sitting there, Meg realized if she hadn't found it by now, she probably wasn't going to be able to on her own. If she was going to find it, she'd need some help. Getting out the phone book, she started flipping through the pages. She'd almost shut the book when she saw the word *Therapist* at the top of a page. In the back of her mind she could hear what her mother would have to say about that. But she ignored her mother's voice and searched until she found an ad she liked.

"A place of hope," she read. Hope. That was what she needed.

"Why are you here?" I asked Meg on her first visit.

"I want you to help me find this house," she said, and smiled. I looked puzzled, and she proceeded to tell me what I've just told you.

Inside the house were all of those special things she'd dreamed of and wanted as a child that somehow never seemed to happen. Inside the house was a father who loved her, a mother who wasn't too busy, a brother who was more than a threat to her place in the family. Inside the house was who she wanted to be, with a family of her own.

Together we began to look for the house. We started from the house she grew up in, through all the houses she'd lived in since then, to the one she was living in now. We talked about what happened in those houses with the people who lived inside them. We talked about why she so desperately wanted the sunny house.

Over the course of our time together, Meg began to feel stronger, to feel better about herself. She decided it wasn't good for her body to drink so much. Even though it was hard to face each day without it, about three months into her search, she resolved to stop drinking. The cigarettes took a little bit longer, but eventually she was able to cut back dramatically in the number she smoked each day and then to quit entirely. For several months, though, she would sit in my office with an unlit cigarette in her hand.

She still hadn't found the house yet, but she decided until she did she could do a better job of taking care of the one she had. Because she had a knack for typing, she put up an ad at the local college to type term papers for money. With that money she hired a house cleaner to come in and help her get a handle on her surroundings. Coming home to a clean house made her feel wonderful, especially since she didn't have to do it all herself. And she found it was easier to keep clean if it started out that way in the first place.

Typing the term papers had rekindled her love of writing. She made suggestions on several papers and was surprised when they were well received. One day when she was at the college putting up more fliers, she decided to sign up for a writing class herself. She decided that maybe she would take enough classes to get another job where she could use her writing more. Although she still went to work doing data entry, she knew now it was only a temporary job while she continued her schooling. Knowing that seemed to make the day go better. Her attitude at work improved, and coworkers began to notice, taking the opportunity to approach her more often.

When she'd given up smoking, Meg had gained several pounds and was having a hard time getting them off. With all the other progress she was experiencing, she didn't want to make a big deal about the weight, but clearly it bothered her. She seemed anxious to lose it but wasn't having the kind of results she'd hoped for. Together we looked at her nutritional patterns and at rebalancing her body after years of unhealthy eating habits. Meg decided that instead of trying to be thin, she'd concentrate on becoming healthy.

As her body and spirit were beginning to heal, Meg's physical presentation changed. The clothes she wore into my office became brighter, more fashionable. She got her hair cut and began to take some care with her appearance. She began to look more her age. Her skin and eyes became brighter. She smiled with more regularity. She actually looked alive!

Her boyfriend left her when she stopped drinking and supplying him with money. He'd started to tear up some of her things as he was leaving, and Meg had to call the police. As they were leading him off, he yelled at her in anger, "I don't need you to tell me what to do!" Hearing that he didn't need her brought up old memories and feelings of despair. It set Meg back for a while, but it forced her to realize she'd been focusing a lot of her attention on the externals. It took some time for her to understand that she was strong enough to deal with the inside.

Meg took a look at her issues of abandonment by her father. She started to deal with the effects of the emotional neglect and favoritism from her mother. Calling and talking with her brother, Rob, she was able to explain to him why she'd always treated him so badly growing up. She told him about the resentment she felt at how her mother seemed to like him more than her. Admitting her anger over her belief that his birth had been responsible for their father leaving was very hard. They were able to talk about things that had happened to them both as children that they had never even acknowledged before. Rob could remember details she didn't and gave a perspective to their life she hadn't seen before.

He was also able to supply Meg with an address and phone number for her father. She didn't know it, but Rob had been keeping in contact with him for several years. Feeling a deep need to be reunited with his father, Rob had sought him out. He hadn't told Meg—afraid she'd think he was taking sides against their mother. Meg wasn't sure she felt as strong as Rob, but she conceded maybe she would write her father a letter just to see what he'd say.

Her mother, on the other hand, all of a sudden had little to say. Although she was genuinely pleased that Meg was doing so well, she was reluctant to talk about the pain she'd caused Meg in the past. Whenever Meg tried to find a way to talk about her feelings, her mother would clam up, not wanting to hear. Meg realized she couldn't wait for her mother to admit to what she'd done, so Meg began to work on forgiving her anyway.

We had been together for over a year when one day I asked Meg what had ever happened to the house. She hadn't mentioned it in months.

She thought for a moment and said, "I'm the house. I don't have to go on looking for it because it was right here all the time." She patted her chest with her hand. "And I'm putting in it all the things I've always wanted. I've never felt better about myself than I do now. I didn't used to think I deserved very much from life, so I chose to put all the good things I wanted into someplace else. Now I know they can be right here inside of me."

This book began with a story about David, the teenager who killed himself because of the despair of his abuse. David gave up hope.

Meg didn't. Through the years of her abuse, Meg kept trying. Kept living. Meg was able to come full circle.

Now it's your turn.

For further assistance, questions, comments, or information on national seminars, please write or call:

The Center for Counseling & Health Resources, Inc.
611 Main P.O. Box 700
Edmonds, WA 98020
(206) 771-5166

Emotional Abuse Questionnaire

Personal History:

_____Female   _____Male

_____Married   (How long?_____)
_____Single   (How long?_____)
_____Divorced (How long?_____)

I feel I've had abusive relationships with the following:

_____Father   _____Coworkers
_____Mother   _____Bosses
_____Both parents   _____Teachers
_____Relatives   _____Classmates
_____A guardian   _____Schoolmates
_____A brother or sister _____Ministers

_____Other (please explain)_____
_____

Answer "Agree," "Disagree," or "Unsure" to the following questions. When a blank line appears, fill in the blank with the most appropriate person or relationship, and then answer the question.

1. I feel I have been emotionally abused in the past.
2. I never felt like my father really approved of me.
3. I had a hard time pleasing my mother while I was growing up.
4. I would often find ways to avoid going home.
5. Growing up I felt disconnected from my parents (caretakers).
6. I rarely felt safe at home as a child.
7. Everyone always wanted me to be more than I was.
8. I wasn't allowed to express my emotions as a child.
9. Others in the family "picked on" me growing up.
10. When I think back on my childhood, more "bad" memories come to mind than "good" memories.
11. I was constantly "lectured to" as a child.
12. Growing up, I was always "wrong," and my _____was always "right."
13. I never felt that my reasons why I did or thought something were taken into account.
14. My _____had a way of always letting me know how stupid I was.
15. I'd often get into shouting matches with them, but I never felt I "won."
16. I seemed to be the "butt" of all the jokes of the family.
17. My _____ always reminded me of how bad I was.
18. Whenever I got into a fight with _____, they'd always bring up everything bad I'd ever done. It seemed like I wasn't just fighting that battle, but refighting every one that had gone on before.

19. Sometimes I felt like running into my room, putting a pillow over my head so I didn't have to listen anymore.
20. My house was rarely peaceful and quiet when I was growing up.
21. I kept trying to please, but nothing seemed to work.
22. Often my _____ yelled instead of spoke to me.
23. I wasn't allowed to question any of my parents (caretakers) decisions growing up.
24. My _____ never actually hit me, but the threat was always implied.
25. My _____'s moods were always up and down. I could never be sure from moment to moment what the mood would be.
26. Growing up I had two "families." The private one was kept secret from what we showed in public.
27. I didn't feel like the favorite child in the family.
28. When I was growing up, my father told me things about my mother that were embarrassing. I felt more like a wife (husband) than a daughter (son).
29. Sometimes I felt more like my _____'s "buddy" than their child.
30. As a child, God was presented as a vengeful superparent who would punish me for the evil inside me.
31. My father never seemed to want to spend any time with me.
32. I was often left alone as a child.
33. My _____ seemed happier when I didn't bother him (her).
34. I often felt like the parent instead of the child.
35. When I finally was able to leave the house, I felt free.
36. I dreaded birthdays and special events because I'd hope my _____ would show up and he (she) wouldn't.
37. Most of the time I felt "on my own."

38. I often felt my _____ would be better off without having to take care of me.
39. I tried to earn affection by doing everything "right."
40. I often felt it was my fault my _____ left.
41. I don't feel people really know "the real me."
42. I often automatically take the blame if something goes wrong.
43. I don't speak up for myself when I'm confronted by someone else.
44. I don't trust my own judgment and will go to others to gain their opinion.
45. I'll go with someone else's opinion, even if it goes against my "gut feeling."
46. My current relationship could be called an abusive one.
47. Even though I'm abused, I feel I love my mate.
48. I really believe my mate will change.
49. I feel like I have to conceal part of me from my mate.
50. It's hard for me to trust and be intimate with another person.
51. I use alcohol/drugs to help get through life.
52. During times of stress, I sometimes have trouble breathing.
53. Sometimes I just feel too tired to cope with life.
54. I experience a lot of digestive problems.
55. I am a bulimic, anorexic, or compulsive overeater.
56. Often I'm anxious for no discernible reason.
57. The doctor can't seem to find out what's wrong with me, even though I go in with specific complaints.
58. I am often incapacitated by migraine headaches.
59. I have experienced brief, intense moments of sheer panic when I'm sure I'm having a heart attack.
60. I have an abnormal fear of normal things.

How to Use This Questionnaire

Go back over this questionnaire and note those questions you said you agreed with. (Take a second look at those you were unsure about and try to pinpoint whether you agree or disagree. If you're still unsure, that's all right, but often saying you are unsure is a way of avoiding having to accept an answer.) Questions 1–10 will help you identify the feelings you had as a child where, in all probability, much of the emotional abuse you have suffered occurred. As you go through these questions and emotions, write down the specific things you are feeling.

Questions 11–40 will help you identify the different types of emotional abuse you have experienced. Remember, just because you experienced emotional abuse in one area, it doesn't mean you can't experience it in another. Emotional abusers will often use a variety of techniques to control those they are abusing. Questions 11–20 deal with verbal emotional abuse. Questions 21–30 cover emotional abuse that is not only conveyed verbally, but also through the actions of others. These last ten questions will guide you to pinpoint feelings of loss and abandonment. They will deal not so much with the actions of others, but with the inactions of others.

Finally, questions 41–60 deal with the repercussions of emotional abuse, either to your emotional self, your physical self, or your relational self. They will help you to identify present conditions and/or behaviors that could have their roots in your past abuse.

Again, here is the breakdown of the questions:

Questions 1–10: Identifying past patterns and feelings.
Questions 11–20: Pinpointing verbally abusive behavior.
Questions 21–30: Pinpointing emotionally abusive behavior.
Questions 31–40: Highlighting abandonment issues.
Questions 41–50: The personal and relational effects.
Questions 51–60: Physical signposts.

Now that you've done all that, ask yourself the following questions:

- Do I believe recovery is possible?
- Am I willing to let go of my past and live for the future?
- Am I ready to forgive and go on?
- Am I ready to believe in myself and my power to change?

For Further Reading

Arterburn, Stephen. *Addicted to "Love": Recovering from Unhealthy Dependencies in Romance, Relationships & Sex.* Ann Arbor, Mich.: Vine Books, 1991.

Backus, William. *Telling Each Other the Truth.* Minneapolis: Bethany House, 1985.

Carder, Dave, Earl Henslin, John Townsend, Henry Cloud, and Alice Brawand. *Secrets of Your Family Tree: Healing for Adult Children of Dysfunctional Families.* Chicago: Moody, 1991.

Carter, Les. *Imperative People: Those Who Must Be in Control.* Nashville: Thomas Nelson, 1991.

Cloud, Henry, and John Townsend. *Boundaries.* Grand Rapids: Zondervan Publishing House, 1992.

Fish, Melinda. *Restoring the Wounded Woman.* Grand Rapids: Chosen Books, 1993.

Fortune, Don and Katie. *Discovering Your God-Given Gifts.* Grand Rapids: Chosen Books, 1987.

Forward, Susan, and Craig Buck. *Toxic Parents: Overcoming Their Hurtful Legacy and Reclaiming Your Life.* New York: Bantam, 1990.

Harley, Willard F., Jr. *His Needs, Her Needs: Building an Affair-proof Marriage.* Grand Rapids: Fleming H. Revell, 1986, 1994.

_____. *Love Busters: Overcoming the Habits That Destroy Romantic Love.* Grand Rapids: Fleming H. Revell, 1992.

Hemfelt, Robert, Frank Minirth, and Paul Meier. *Love Is a Choice.* Nashville: Thomas Nelson, 1989.

Hendrix, Harville, *Getting the Love You Want: A Guide for Couples.* New York: HarperPerennial, 1990.

Hershey, Terry. *Intimacy: The Longing of Every Human Heart.* Eugene, Oreg.: Harvest House, 1988.

Hillerstrom, P. Roger. *Your Family Voyage.* Grand Rapids: Fleming H. Revell, 1993.

McGinnis, Alan Loy. *The Friendship Factor.* Minneapolis: Augsburg, 1979.

_____. *Confidence: How to Succeed at Being Yourself.* Minneapolis: Augsburg, 1987.

Parrott, L. *Love's Unseen Enemy.* Grand Rapids: Zondervan Publishing House, 1994.

Rainey, Dennis and Barbara. *Building Your Mate's Self-Esteem.* Nashville: Thomas Nelson, 1986.

Seamands, David A. *Healing for Damaged Emotions: Recovering from the Memories That Cause Our Pain.* Wheaton: Victor Books, 1991.

Snyder, Chuck and Barb. *Incompatibility: Grounds for a Great Marriage.* Sisters, Oreg.: Questar Publishers, 1988.

Stoop, David, and James Masteller. *Forgiving Our Parents, Forgiving Ourselves.* Ann Arbor, Mich.: Vine Books, 1992.

Townsend, John. *Hiding from Love: How to Change Withdrawal Patterns That Isolate and Imprison You.* Colorado Springs: NavPress, 1991.

Williams, Pat and Jill. *Rekindled.* Grand Rapids: Fleming H. Revell, 1985.

Wright, Norman. *Making Peace with Your Past.* Grand Rapids: Fleming H. Revell, 1985.